Beauty by THE BOOK

Becoming a Biblically Beautiful Woman

A 7-Week Study of Proverbs

by Laurie Cole

Production Coordinator • Pam Henderson
Layout and Design • Pam Henderson
Editors • Robin Cook, Pat Habashy
Cover Design and Graphic Artwork • Julie Riley, J. Riley Creative, LLC, Houston, Texas
Photography • Don and Mary Carico, Lakewood Photography, League City, Texas

Priority Ministries
Encouraging Women to Give God Glory & Priority

Priority Ministries
www.priorityministries.org

Dedication

To my biblically beautiful friends,
Janet, Pam, Shanda, Debbie, Jan, Courtney and Stephanie,
the staff of Priority Ministries

Acknowledgements

Priority Ministries was blessed and privileged to pilot *Beauty by The Book* in 2007 with the wonderful women of the **M & M (Mary & Martha) Bible study at Sagemont Church in Houston, Texas**. Each week these women patiently and graciously filled out evaluation forms providing us with invaluable information that enabled us to revise and improve this study. As you look over the list of their names, we hope you'll thank the Lord for the blessing they've been to us and to you.

Katia Banfield, Director/Coordinator
Pat Godwin, Assistant Coordinator

Linda Adams
Markie Aguirre
Rosa Linda Aguirre
Kay Ali
Kathy Allegra
Pamela Allen
Barbara Ames
Angela Amyx
Sheila Anderson
Denise Bacon
Katia Banfield
Barbara Barker
Bonnye Barnes
Gloria Barton
Brenda Berlingeri
Jodie Boening
Brenda Bondy
Paula Box
Kathi Bradley
Crystal Brinker
Debi Brown
Diane Burcham
Joy Burkhalter
Vanessa Byerly
Kim Campbell
Robin Canfield
Tami Carroll
Phyllis Carroll
Eleanore Cassady
Sherial Caswell
Shelia Cheatwood
Vicki Cizmar
Dede Clark
Anita Clark
Carolyn Coleman
Sharon Colligan
Vicki Collins
Juanita Cook
Ruby Cook
Vivianne Culpepper

Connie Curtis
Rachelle Davenport
Libby Davis
Estella Davis
Debbie Davis
Karen Dean
Jo Ann Delgado Puente
Glenda Dewbre
Lydia Dobbs
Jill Dorsett
Mable Dyer
Patricia Ehman
Denise Elliott
Beverly Ewald
Debbie Finn
Leticia Flores
Anita Fontenot
Katie Ford
Kristen Forsyth
Teri Fowle
Relda Freeman
Salome Garcia
Betty Garner
Valerie Garza
Susan Goddard
Kathy Gouger
Trace Griesel
Dottie Halstead
Lisa Harris
Vicki Harvey
Jeanne Harvey
Kathy Hawkins
Darla Haygood
Carol Haynes
Becky Hazen
Nancy Heckel
Deirdre Hedrick
Tamara Helms
Irene Hendrickson
Ashley Higgins

Kathy Hilburn
Cathy Hipps
Donna Hodges
Mary Ellen Holmes
Bonnie Holsomback
Heather Houston
Bobbi Huber
Renee Human
Betty Elaine Hunter
Frances Jackson
Sandra Jackson
Virginia Jones
Mary Jones
Katherine Kieselhorst
Linda Lakeness
Sheila Lalumandier
Liane Lay
Carrie Lee
Nian Lening
Edna Lin
Lucinda Long
Vicky Lucchese
Jean Maciukiewicz
Linda Mahany
Mary Marcaccio
Renea Marchi
Jean Marlowe
Linda Massey
Diane Matzka
Janice McClure
Merinell McCollum
Brenda McDonald
Laura McGee
Kakie McKinney
Debbie Melson
Rachel Montemayor
Tricia Moore
Sue Moore
Terri Morrison
Mary Muguerza

Jan Myers
Mica Nagle
Joyce Nesby
Dana Nesmith
Georjean Nixon
Kelly Nolin
Joyce Nylund
Mayra Painter
Kathy Perry
Erika Perry
Myrna Peters
Martha Pitts
Eileen Ponton
LaNell Pounds
Leah Pounds
Nena Powell
Patricia Ragan
Donna Reeves
Cindy Reeves
Patricia Reeves
Ana Reyes
Sharon Rigsby
Lydia Riley
Ruthie Rogers
Claudia Sabella
Nancy Sammons
Brooke Santos
Becky Sayers
Nadine Schliesky
LeeAnn Schultz
Joyce Shannon
Frances Sherer
Susan Sheridan
Tammy Sidney
Lynda Simmons
Christy Simmons
Pat Sims
Beth Sinclair
Tamara Skeete
Vickie Smith
Rebecca Smith

Jan Smith
Alma Smith
Terry Smith
Sandy Smith
Janie Southard
Renee Stapp
Gwen Staton
Maria Steel
Karen Steen
Heather Steen
Shanda Terry
Sharon Thompson
Debbie Todd
Britney Todd
Kay Tucker
Lindsey Uriquia
Elizabeth VanEtten
Lisa VanEtten
Wanda Veltman
Donna Vogel
Donna Vogt
Kay Walker
Charlotte Walker
Jana Walsh
Zaida Walters
Rose Marie Walton
Carol Weld
Jan Wilks
Charlyn Williams
Penny Williams
Beth Williams
Janice Willis
Carol Wilson
Greta Wilson
Jean Womack
Suzanne Wright
Cyndy Young
Barbara Young
Cynthia Yzquierdo
Clara Zamora
Diane Zimmerman

About THE STUDY

This Bible study is a simple tool to help you discover life-changing truths from God's Word. Think of this workbook as a chisel and your Bible as a gold mine. Each day you'll "dig-in" to God's Word to discover precious treasures that will enrich your life for His glory (Psalm 19:9–10, 119:162). Homework for this study will require approximately 20 minutes per day, five days per week.

The Holy Spirit will be your Divine Tutor throughout this study (John 16:13), and prayer will be essential in facilitating your sensitivity to His leadership. Therefore, a *pray* paragraph is included at the beginning of each day's homework. At the conclusion of your daily study, you'll be encouraged to record any insights the Holy Spirit has shown you in a brief *reflect* section.

A good translation of the Bible will be essential as you use this study. The *New Living Translation,* Second Edition, the *New International Version,* the *New American Standard Bible,* the *New King James Version,* or the *King James Version* are all very accurate translations and are highly recommended. In this study, the author will primarily use the *New Living Translation.*

About THE AUTHOR

Laurie Cole is the Founder and President of Priority Ministries, a ministry dedicated to encouraging and equipping women to love God most and seek Him first. Raised in a strong Christian home, Laurie became a Christian at an early age. But in her early twenties, God tested and taught her the importance of truly giving Him priority in her life.

In 1985, Laurie enrolled in an in-depth women's Bible study. Encouraged by the older women who led the study, Laurie received training and began teaching and leading a group where God affirmed His call upon her life to teach. For over 20 years, Laurie has taught dozens of Bible studies, spoken at numerous women's events and conferences, and is the author of two in-depth Bible studies: *There Is A Season* and *The Temple*. Her passion for God and hunger for His Word continues to grow.

A minister's wife, Laurie and her husband, Bill, serve the Lord at Sagemont Church in Houston, Texas, where he is the Associate Pastor of Worship and Praise. They have been married for 37 years and have three sons (David, Kevin, and J.J.), two beloved daughters-in-law (Stephanie and Rachael), and four glorious grandchildren (Ezra, Juliette, Caroline, and Aubrey).

Table of CONTENTS

Introduction TO THE STUDY

I have a confession to make. If you'd told me a couple of years ago that I would be writing a Bible study about beauty, I would have shaken my head, squinted my eyes and replied with absolute disdain, "No way. A Bible study about beauty? How shallow." Wrong!

Not only was I wrong in thinking I would never write a study about beauty, I was even more wrong in my attitude toward the topic. So what changed my condescending outlook, and who convinced me of my wrong-headed point of view? God. And now I know what He knew all along: beauty is no shallow subject. In fact, God wants all of His daughters to be beautiful—biblically beautiful, that is.

In today's culture, beauty is an idol worshipped and pursued by multitudes of women both young and old. Biblical beauty, however, is vastly different from worldly beauty; but you probably already know that. What you may not know, however, is just how much you have been influenced by the world's definition and beliefs about beauty. Therefore, before you even begin this study, I must warn you:

This Bible study contains material that may be deemed offensive by women (maybe even you), but I'm writing it anyway. Study at your own risk.

OK, I wrote that little warning with a smile on my face, but I really do want to caution you about something: God's Word is powerful. It has the power to reprove and correct, to judge and offend, and to pierce us to the very quick of our hearts (2 Timothy 3:16, Hebrews 4:12). And believe me, I can testify to this power firsthand. One of the very first reproofs I experienced as I was researching this study was about how much time and money I have spent worshipping the idol of worldly beauty. Ouch!

My research for this study also confirmed the enormous chasm that exists between God's standards and the popular standards of today's world. When contrasted with the prevailing philosophies and "enlightened" beliefs of our current culture, God's Word seems (I said "*seems*," not "*is*") old-fashioned and out-dated. Therefore, adopting God's definition of beauty will require us to swim against some very strong cultural currents.

Like the constantly changing hemlines of today's fashions, the world's definition of beauty will continuously evolve. But one thing will never change: God's Word—The Book. More relevant today than the latest issue of *Vogue*. More liberating than the most recent reinvention of feminism. God's Word is timeless, transformational, and true. Study its standards, practice its principles and, my beloved sister, you will become a true beauty—a biblically beautiful woman of God.

Your Sister,

Laurie

"The grass withers, and the flowers fade, but the Word of our God stands forever."
—Isaiah 40:8 *NLT*

Introductory Week • PHYSICAL BEAUTY VS. BIBLICAL BEAUTY

Physical Beauty...

1) Is _____-_____. *Ezekiel 16:4–13*

2) Is _____-_____. *Ezekiel 16:14*

3) Is _____-_____. *Ezekiel 16:15*

4) Is _____ _____. *Ezekiel 16:15–18*

Biblical Beauty...

1) Is _____-_____. *1 Peter 3:3–4*

2) Is _____ and _____. *1 Peter 3:3–4*

3) Is _____ in God's sight. *1 Peter 3:3–4*

4) Is _____ and _____. *1 Peter 3:3–4*

> One thing I have asked from the LORD, that I shall seek:
> that I may dwell in the house of the LORD all the days of my life,
> to behold the beauty of the LORD and to meditate in His temple.
> —Psalm 27:4

Question: How can you become a biblically beautiful woman of God?

Answer: By _____ God and
_____ the standard of His Word.

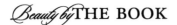

Week One • FIVE BEAUTY DOS & DON'TS

This week I will be introducing you to five women. These five females all make their home in the Book of Proverbs. For the next six weeks, we will be spending quite a bit of time with them as we learn how to become biblically beautiful women of God. But before you meet them, you need to know something: not all of these women qualify as true biblical beauties.

Let me explain. You've probably seen those "beauty do" and "beauty don't" photos in the fashion magazines haven't you? Well, some of the five women you're about to meet are biblical "beauty dos," but others are biblical "beauty don'ts." And trust me, you won't have any trouble telling which ones are which.

So, c'mon. Let's head to Proverbs—our home for the next six weeks.

P.S. Don't worry about coming down with a bad case of "cabin fever" from being stuck inside Proverbs for six weeks. We'll get out often and visit women in other books of the Bible, too. I've even arranged for us to take a few topical tours through the Scriptures together. Girl, these six weeks are going fly by!

• • • • •

DAY ONE

I almost forgot to tell you, there is a sixth "woman" we'll be getting to know in Proverbs. Her name is Wisdom. All throughout Proverbs, the author uses the female pronoun "she" to refer to wisdom. Don't you just love that! But let's not get too carried away, because there is a seventh "woman" mentioned in the Proverbs, and her name is Folly.

This sixth "woman"—Wisdom—will be the focus of our daily *pray* time. If you want to become a biblically beautiful woman as I do, it is essential that we get to know Ms. Wisdom well.

1. Good news! Wisdom is available to everyone who needs it. And we *all* need it. James 1:5 promises that "if any of you lack wisdom, let him ask of God who gives to all men generously and without reproach and it will be given to him" (*NASB*). Begin your first day of study by bowing your head and praising God as the source of true wisdom. Ask Him to pour out His wisdom upon you and make you wise.

> *Wisdom shouts in the streets.*
> *She cries out in the public square...*
> *"Come here and listen to me!*
> *I'll pour out the spirit of wisdom*
> *upon you and make you wise."*
> —Proverbs 1:20–23

2. Brace yourself. You're about to meet Beauty #1, the first female mentioned in Proverbs, and she's a doozy. Allow me to introduce you to the **Immoral Woman** as you read Proverbs 5:3–6:

> ³ *For the lips of an adulteress [woman] drip honey,*
> *and her speech is smoother than oil;*
> ⁴ *but in the end she is bitter as gall,*
> *sharp as a double-edged sword.*
> ⁵ *Her feet go down to death;*
> *her steps lead straight to the grave.*
> ⁶ *She gives no thought to the way of life;*
> *her paths are crooked, but she knows it not.*
> —Proverbs 5:3–6 *NIV*

3. Based upon Proverbs 5:3–6, please answer the following questions about the Immoral Woman:

   a. What's the very first thing you learned about her (verse 3)?

b. Excluding the language used within the text, what other words or phrases might describe her manner of speech and method of communication?

c. What kind of first impression does she usually make?

d. According to verse 4, what will others eventually discover about her, and when will they discover it?

e. What is her final destination and why (verses 5–6)?

You've just experienced your first encounter with the Immoral Woman, but it won't be your last. Next week, you'll study her extensively, and you may be surprised to learn that five passages and one entire chapter of Proverbs are devoted to her. She gets more press and attention than any of the other four women we'll be studying. And I think you'll agree that she certainly gets the most press in today's world, which leads me to ask this:

4. What kind of reputation does the Immoral Woman have in today's culture?

5. You probably have seen the Immoral Woman many times in many places, but if you had to name the top three places you most consistently see her in our culture, where would they be?

6. Why do you think five passages and one chapter of Proverbs are devoted to the Immoral Woman? In other words, why would God want us to get to know her so well?

7. A few minutes ago, you prayed and asked God for wisdom. What wisdom has He given you through your study today? And if you're a mom, how could Proverbs 5:3-6 be particularly useful to you?

_____

_____

_____

_____

• • • • •

DAY TWO

1. Tuning into God has never been more difficult than it is today. Hearing His still, small voice over the constant cacophony of technology—ringing cell phones, busy blackberries, and 24/7 access to the worldwide web—is no small feat. But by daily and deliberately making today's Proverb a priority, you can still hear God speak. So, right now, tune out the racket around you, and tune in to God and His wisdom through prayer.

> *Tune your ears to wisdom, and*
> *concentrate on understanding.*
> —Proverbs 2:2

Today you will meet two more women from Proverbs: the Indiscreet Woman and the Irritating Woman. I know. They probably don't sound like the kind of women who can teach us much about biblical beauty, but here's a great passage to remind us why we can't afford to ignore them:

> *All Scripture is inspired by God and is useful to teach us what is true*
> *and to make us realize what is wrong in our lives. It straightens us out*
> *and teaches us to do what is right. It is God's way of preparing us in*
> *every way, fully equipped for every good thing God wants us to do.*
> —2 Timothy 3:16–17

2. Keeping 2 Timothy 3:16–17 in mind, meet Beauty #2 by reading the following scripture:

> *A woman who is beautiful but lacks discretion*
> *is like a gold ring in a pig's snout.*
> — Proverbs 11:22

Wow! That's one blunt verse, huh? While Beauty #2, the **Indiscreet Woman**, may be rich in the looks department, her lack of discretion is her ruin. Thus, one of the primary principles we can learn from her is that no amount of make-up, spa treatments, Botox® injections, or even plastic surgery can cover up a deficit of discretion. So, what exactly is discretion, and how can we get it? In a couple of weeks, we'll study discretion in detail; but for now, find out a few basics about it by completing the following assignments:

3. Look up the following words in any dictionaries (secular or biblical) you have, and record their definitions in the space provided:

NOTE: Please feel free to search for these definitions online. The *Merriam-Webster* dictionary at <u>www.m-w.com</u> or *Dictionary.Com* at <u>www.dictionary.com</u> are both excellent resources.

a. discretion

b. discreet

c. indiscreet

d. prudent (often used as a synonym for "discretion")

4. Name one or two discreet or prudent women you have known, and briefly explain how or why they exemplify discretion and prudence.

5. Discretion is a "must have" for every biblically beautiful woman. Discover how to get it by reading Proverbs 1:1–5 and answering the following questions:

   a. Who wrote the Book of Proverbs?

   b. Why did he write it (verses 2–5)?

   c. According to this passage, how can we obtain discretion?

We need to move along now and meet Beauty #3, the **Irritating Woman**. We won't spend much time with her today, but that's OK. A little time with her goes a long way!

6. Meet Beauty #3 by reading the following scriptures:

    > *It is better to live alone in the corner of an attic*
    > *than with a contentious wife in a lovely home.*
    > —Proverbs 21:9

    > *It is better to live alone in the desert*
    > *than with a crabby complaining wife.*
    > — Proverbs 21:19

    We've all met this woman before haven't we? But let's be honest: at times, we've all been this woman, too. And while these verses may specifically apply to married women, you and I both know that crabbiness does not discriminate. Anyone (married or single, young or old, male or female, Christian or non-Christian) can exhibit the classic symptoms of what I call "3C Syndrome": (1) Contentiousness, (2) Crabbiness, with frequent bouts of (3) Complaining.

    Fortunately, 3C is not generally contagious, and there is a cure (we'll uncover it in the weeks ahead). But for now, let's focus on the primary and possible long-term effects of 3C.

7. According to Proverbs 21:9 and 19:

    a. How does 3C affect our relationships with others?

    b. What potential long-term effects could 3C cause in our relationships with others?

8. Might *you* have a mild (or possibly serious) case of 3C? Take a quick check-up by circling the word that most accurately completes each of the following sentences:

    a. My friends and family would probably say that I am crabby:

    rarely   occasionally   frequently

    b. My friends and family would probably say that I complain:

    rarely   occasionally   frequently

    c. My friends and family would probably say that I am usually:

    easygoing   a little high-maintenance   downright difficult

    d. My friends and family would probably say that my words arc usually:

    encouraging and kind   sweet and sour   negative and nagging

9. If your check-up revealed a possible case of 3C, a quick dose of wisdom and instruction from Proverbs should ease some of your symptoms until we can study the cure in the weeks ahead. Begin applying the following verses to your life as often and as liberally as needed:

    > *Don't talk too much, for it fosters sin.*
    > *Be sensible and turn off the flow!*
    > —Proverbs 10:19

    > *Kind words are like honey—*
    > *Sweet to the soul and healthy for the body.*
    > —Proverbs 16:24

10. Do you agree that there is a lot we can learn from the two women we've met today? What insights has the Holy Spirit taught you today through the Indiscreet Woman and the Irritating Woman?

reflect

_____

_____

_____

_____

_____

DAY THREE

1. The fear of the Lord is a very positive and beneficial thing. It is where true wisdom begins. So what exactly is it? Very simply, the fear of the Lord is reverence for God that results in obedience to God. It is both attitude (reverence) and action (obedience); and when you put them together, you get wisdom! Before you begin today's study, submit yourself in reverence before God in prayer, and commit to obey Him. Then watch for wisdom to show up.

> *Fear of the LORD is the beginning of wisdom.*
> *Knowledge of the Holy One results in understanding.*
> —Proverbs 9:10

2. I am very excited today to introduce you to Beauty #4. This woman bears no resemblance to the three women you have previously met in Proverbs—thank goodness! So, without further adieu, it is my privilege now to introduce you to Beauty #4, the **Captivating Woman**:

> ¹⁸ *Let your wife be a fountain of blessing for you.*
> *Rejoice in the wife of your youth.*
> ¹⁹ *She is a loving doe, a graceful deer.*
> *Let her breasts satisfy you always.*
> *May you always be captivated by her love.*
> —Proverbs 5:18–19

The first seven chapters of Proverbs are specifically addressed from a father (Solomon, the author of the Proverbs) to his son. In the Proverbs 5 passage you just read, the father is exhorting his son to seek love and sexual satisfaction within the bounds of a monogamous marriage to a captivating woman.

3. According to Proverbs 5:18–19, what are the characteristics of a Captivating Woman?

4. The bonuses and benefits to the husband of a Captivating Woman are pretty obvious, but is he the sole beneficiary in this marriage? In other words, are there also benefits for the Captivating Woman and for the overall marital relationship? Ponder these questions, and explain your answer.

Every scripture in the Bible is inspired by God. He is the ultimate Author of every passage and verse (2 Peter 1:21). Therefore, when we read a sensual passage like Proverbs 5:18–19, God Himself is instructing and encouraging us to enjoy freely the pleasures of sexual intimacy within marriage. And Proverbs 5:18–19 is really quite tame compared to other biblical passages. Just wait until we study Song of Solomon in Week 5!

5. There is one final verse I'd like for you to look up today: Genesis 2:25. Read it (in fact, go ahead and read verses 21–25); then write verse 25, word-for-word, in the space below.

6. How does Genesis 2:25 parallel Proverbs 5:18–19?

7. As a woman (or as a wife), how has God spoken to your heart through His Word today?

_____

_____

_____

_____

reflect

· · · · ·

DAY FOUR

pray

1. What's at the top of your "want list"? You know what I mean— most of us have a list in our head of things we'd really like to have. But do you know what should always be at the very top? Wisdom. Take today's passage before the Lord in prayer, and commit to giving it priority on your "want list".

> *Choose (wisdom's) instruction rather than silver,*
> *and knowledge over pure gold.*
> *For wisdom is far more valuable than rubies.*
> *Nothing you desire can be compared with it.*
> —Proverbs 8:10–11

2. Thus far, you've met the first four women from Proverbs. Are you ready to meet our final beauty, Beauty #5? You've probably heard about her before. Hands down, she's the most well-known woman in Proverbs. Prepare to be dazzled as you meet Beauty #5: the **Ideal Woman**.

Proverbs 31:10–31

¹⁰ *Who can find a virtuous and capable wife? She is worth more than precious rubies.*

¹¹ *Her husband can trust her, and she will greatly enrich his life.*

¹² *She will not hinder him but help him all her life.*

¹³ *She finds wool and flax and busily spins it.*

¹⁴ *She is like a merchant's ship; she brings her food from afar.*

¹⁵ *She gets up before dawn to prepare breakfast for her household and plan the day's work for her servant girls.*

¹⁶ *She goes out to inspect a field and buys it; with her earnings she plants a vineyard.*

¹⁷ *She is energetic and strong, a hard worker.*

¹⁸ *She watches for bargains; her lights burn late into the night.*

¹⁹ *Her hands are busy spinning thread, her fingers twisting fiber.*

²⁰ *She extends a helping hand to the poor and opens her arms to the needy.*

²¹ *She has no fear of winter for her household because all of them have warm clothes.*

²² *She quilts her own bedspreads. She dresses like royalty in gowns of finest cloth.*

²³ *Her husband is well known, for he sits in the council meeting with the other civic leaders.*

²⁴ *She makes belted linen garments and sashes to sell to the merchants.*

²⁵ *She is clothed with strength and dignity, and she laughs with no fear of the future.*

²⁶ *When she speaks, her words are wise, and kindness is the rule when she gives instructions.*

²⁷ *She carefully watches all that goes on in her household and does not have to bear the consequences of laziness.*

²⁸ *Her children stand and bless her. Her husband praises her:*

²⁹ *"There are many virtuous and capable women in the world, but you surpass them all!"*

³⁰ *Charm is deceptive, and beauty does not last; but a woman who fears the Lord will be greatly praised.*

³¹ *Reward her for all she has done. Let her deeds publicly declare her praise.*

After reading such an extensive passage extolling the virtues of the Ideal Woman, the phrase "total package" comes to my mind. Wow! This woman's got it all and, furthermore, she's got it all *very* together.

But let me tell you something totally liberating that I learned several years ago about Proverbs 31:10–31: this passage is *not* describing a day in the life of the Ideal Woman (thank you, Lord!). Instead, this passage paints a panoramic picture of her life and career as a wife, mother, minister, and entrepreneur. So, if you are dismayed instead of dazzled by this passage, take heart. The Ideal woman didn't arrive at "Ideal-ness" in a day, or a month, or even a year. But make no mistake, she *did* arrive. And so should we.

3. Proverbs 31:10–31 details many of the qualities, characteristics, and accomplishments of the Ideal Woman. As you review the passage, which qualities, characteristics and accomplishments do you most appreciate and desire for your own life?

4. How does Beauty #5 compare or contrast with:

   a. Beauty #1: The Immoral Woman (pages 3–6)

   b. Beauty #2: The Indiscreet Woman (pages 6–8)

   c. Beauty #3: The Irritating Woman (pages 9–10)

   d. Beauty #4: The Captivating Woman (pages 11–13)

5. As you take a panoramic look at your own life and Christian walk, what spiritual growth have you seen in your character, service, and relationships? Record your answer by praising and thanking God for some of the specific ways you've most recently seen Him at work in your life.

_____

_____

_____

_____

_____

• • • • •

DAY FIVE

1. The Book of Proverbs is a collection of wise sayings written and edited by Solomon to teach us how to live wise, godly lives (Proverbs 1:1–6). As you've already seen, it's an extremely practical book. But a proverb is not a promise. While each saying and proverb is generally true, there are exceptions (one of which you're about to see. We've all known wise people who died young). Still, the benefits of wise living are obvious. As you conclude the first week of your study, pray and thank God for the wisdom you've already gleaned and for the benefits you've already seen.

Wisdom will multiply your days and add years to your life.
If you become wise, you will be the one to benefit.
If you scorn wisdom, you will be the one to suffer.
—Proverbs 9:11–12

This week, you've briefly met the five females from Proverbs. In the next five weeks, these women will teach us the basics of biblical beauty. But before we conclude this first week of study, there's one very important thing we must do: we need to define biblical beauty.

2. According to the following passages, what are the scriptural principles and qualities of biblical beauty? Record your answers in the space provided.

    a.   1 Samuel 16:7

    b.   1 Peter 3:3–4

3. The prophet Isaiah foretold Christ's coming in great detail. He even provided us with information about Jesus' physical appearance and beauty. Read Isaiah 53:2, and record what you learn about the beauty of Christ. (**NOTE: the "He" in this verse refers to Christ.**)

4. Using all of the scriptural information you acquired in Questions 2 and 3, define biblical beauty in your own words by completing the following sentence:

    Biblical beauty is…

5. Based upon everything you've studied this week about biblical beauty, check the box that correctly describes each of our 5 Beauties from the Proverbs:

    a. The Immoral Woman is a: ❑ Biblical Beauty Do
                                             ❑ Biblical Beauty Don't

    b. The Indiscreet Woman is a: ❑ Biblical Beauty Do
                                             ❑ Biblical Beauty Don't

    c. The Irritating Woman is a: ❑ Biblical Beauty Do
                                             ❑ Biblical Beauty Don't

    d. The Captivating Woman is a: ❑ Biblical Beauty Do
                                             ❑ Biblical Beauty Don't

    e. The Ideal Woman is a: ❑ Biblical Beauty Do
                                             ❑ Biblical Beauty Don't

6. Do you know someone who is a Biblical Beauty Do? Did any familiar faces come to mind as you reviewed the Biblical Beauty Dos in this week's lesson? If so, then take a minute right now to pick up the phone or drop them a note. Thank and affirm them for the godly example they have been in your life. Trust me. You will make their day and bless them immeasurably.

7. As you reflect on what you've learned and studied this week, what primary principle has the Lord most impressed upon your heart and life?

reflect

_____

_____

_____

_____

On June 14, 2007, a well-known biblical beauty died. After many years of declining health, Ruth Bell Graham (wife of evangelist Billy Graham) went to be with the Lord at the age of 87. At her funeral, her children remembered her as funny, feisty, and full of love for Jesus and His Word.

Although he was not expected nor scheduled to speak, Billy Graham (impelled, no doubt, by the Spirit) rose to his feet and spoke at Ruth's service. In his brief address, he recalled the previous evening when he'd visited the funeral home to see Ruth one last time. Then he said, "I wish you could look into the casket because she's so beautiful." Ruth's beauty transcended even death.

In a world that worships physical, temporal beauty, the life and death of Ruth Bell Graham proves that biblical beauty is timeless and eternal. It has the awesome power to grow and intensify even as our bodies weaken and fade. It is the amazing promise to all who love the Lord and live His Word. It is real beauty. It is rare beauty. It is beauty by The Book.

Week One • BIBLICAL BEAUTY ACCORDING TO PROVERBS

Background on Proverbs:

1) *Author of Proverbs:* _____ 1:1, 1 Kings 3:5–12

2) *Purpose of Proverbs* (1:1–6): To give wisdom, discipline, understanding, prudence, knowledge and discretion to the _____ AND the _____.

3) *Primary Principle of Proverbs* (1:7): The fear of the Lord is the _____/_____ of wisdom and knowledge.

   The fear of the Lord = _____ **for God**

   that results in _____ to God.

4) *Present Day Proverb:*

   " _____. "

   Our Goal as we study Proverbs: To _____ **AND** _____/_____ **God better.**

Biblical Beauty Dos: *According to Proverbs:*

1) _____ and _____. (Beauty Don't #1: The Immoral Woman)

2) _____ and _____. (Beauty Don't #2: The Indiscreet Woman)

3) _____ and _____. (Beauty Don't #3: The Irritating Woman)

4) _____ and _____. (Beauty Do #1: The Captivating Woman)

5) _____ and _____. (Beauty Do #2: The Ideal Woman)

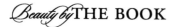

Week Two • THE IMMORAL WOMAN

As I write this lesson, I have a specific group of women on my heart: moms and their pre-teen and teenage daughters. But if you're thinking, "Laurie, I don't fit the mother/daughter crowd," let me assure you that God will use His Word to speak to all of us this week.

The culture has changed so much since I was a teenager. Visit any mall and you'll see teenage cleavage everywhere, thongs (and I don't mean flip flops) peeking out of low-rise jeans, and teenage girls openly shopping with their teenage boyfriends in Victoria's Secret stores. The evidence and effects of the Immoral Woman's influence upon our culture, and specifically our teenagers, is epidemic.

But the Immoral Woman hasn't just captured our culture. She's actively seducing the church as well. Using television, movies, magazines and the internet, she seeks to desensitize us to her permissive, provocative lifestyle. She coaxes us to compromise our own standards *and* to give in to our daughters who protest and proclaim, "Mom, everybody dresses like this. It's no big deal. And besides, if a guy has a problem with the way I'm dressed, then he shouldn't be looking. Just because I'm a Christian doesn't mean I can't look hot."

Battle-weary moms unite! Married women, single women, old and young women alike, rise up! It's time to declare war on the aggressive, destructive, power-hungry presence of the Immoral Woman in our lives. We must arm ourselves with the Truth and send her back to the Satanic pit she came from. And by the authority of God's Word I can promise you this: Victory is ours for the taking.

> *You are from God, little children, and have overcome them;*
> *because greater is He who is in you than he who is in the world.*
> —1 John 4:4 *NASB*

DAY ONE

1. Begin your study this week in prayer by asking God to search your heart and reveal all the impurities in your life. Be still. Allow God to speak to you. Take time to confess each sin to Him, and receive His cleansing and forgiveness. Commit to complete repentance, and ask God for wisdom to keep you pure.

> *Wisdom will save you from the immoral woman,*
> *from the flattery of the adulterous woman."*
> —Proverbs 2:16

The Immoral Woman has become so mainstream and so popular these days that some people don't even recognize her for the heartbreaking, troublemaking, home-wrecking seductress that she is. So this week, we're going to expose her by shining the light of God's Word directly on her.

As Christians, we must not underestimate the peril the Immoral Woman poses to us and to our families. This gal is dangerous. Thankfully, God's Word enables us to identify her so that we can train our sons and daughters to avoid her and warn our husbands as well. But there is another reason we need to take a long, hard scriptural look at the Immoral Woman: we must make sure that our lives bear absolutely no resemblance whatsoever to hers.

2. Please read Proverbs 2:16–19, and answer the following questions:

   a. What are some of the characteristics of the Immoral Woman?

   b. How does she treat her husband, and what does that reveal about her character?

    c.   How dangerous is she?

3.   Last week, when you first met the Immoral Woman, you read Proverbs 5:3–6. But let's revisit that passage (this time using the New Living Translation) to see how it parallels Proverbs 2:16–19. Please read Proverbs 5:3–6, and answer the questions that follow:

> ³ *The lips of an immoral woman are as sweet as honey,*
> *and her mouth is smoother than oil.*
> ⁴ *but the result is bitter as poison,*
> *sharp as a double-edged sword.*
> ⁵ *Her feet go down to death;*
> *her steps lead straight to the grave.*
> ⁶ *She does not care about the path to life.*
> *She staggers down a crooked trail and*
> *doesn't even realize where it leads.*
>   —Proverbs 5:3–6

    a.   How does the description of the Immoral Woman in Proverbs 5 compare with the Proverbs 2 passage? What similarities do you see?

    b. According to verse 6, what does she neither care nor think about?

c. How does verse 6 relate to verse 5?

4. Proverbs 30:20 further reveals the character and attitude of the Immoral Woman. Part of this verse (from the *NLT*) is recorded for you. Use your Bible to record the final words of this verse in the blank provided.

    Equally amazing is how an adulterous woman can satisfy her sexual appetite, shrug her shoulders, and then say,

    " _____ "

    —Proverbs 30:20

5. What does the Immoral Woman's statement in Proverbs 30:20 reveal about her character, and why is this so dangerous to others?

6. What insights has the Holy Spirit given you through your study today? How can you use what you've learned today?

    _____

    _____ *reflect*

    _____

    _____

DAY TWO

1. As you begin today's study in prayer, acknowledge your need for wisdom before God. Tell Him that you recognize He is your source for wisdom, and ask Him to speak to you through the pages of His Word.

   For the Lord grants wisdom!
   From his mouth come knowledge and understanding.
   —Proverbs 2:6

Lights, camera, action! The passage we're about to read is written so vividly that it's almost like watching a movie. It is the longest, most descriptive passage ever written about the Immoral Woman in the Scriptures, and it sheds more light on her ways and wiles than any of the passages we studied yesterday. Get ready for an Academy-award-winning performance by a woman playing her part to perfection, our Beauty Don't #1, the **Immoral Woman**.

2. Your primary assignment today is to read and examine Proverbs 7:4–27 as you:

   • Circle any words or phrases used to describe the Immoral Woman.

   • Make notes of your own observations about her and the way she operates in the margins beside this passage.

To help you get started, I've already circled a couple of words, and you'll also see one of my notes in the margin. I encourage you to fill up the margins with your insights and personal "takes" on the Immoral Woman. The margins of my own copy of this passage are full of notes I've taken, and I have to tell you: there's something very empowering about exposing this woman for who she really is.

Proverbs 7:4-27 *(NLT)*

⁴ *Love wisdom like a sister; make insight a beloved member of your family.*

⁵ *Let them hold you back from an affair with an immoral woman, from listening to the* (*flattery*) *of an adulterous woman.*

⁶ *I was looking out the window of my house one day*

⁷ *and saw a simpleminded young man who lacked common sense.*

⁸ *He was crossing the street near the house of an immoral woman. He was strolling down the path by her house*

⁹ *at twilight, as the day was fading, as the dark of night set in.*

¹⁰ *The woman approached him,* (*dressed seductively*) *and sly of heart.*

She makes the first move; she's one aggressive chick.

¹¹ *She was the brash, rebellious type who never stays at home.*

¹² *She is often seen in the streets and markets, soliciting at every corner.*

¹³ *She threw her arms around him and kissed him, and with a brazen look she said,*

¹⁴ *"I've offered my sacrifices and just finished my vows.*

¹⁵ *It's you I was looking for! I came out to find you, and here you are!*

¹⁶ *My bed is spread with colored sheets of finest linen imported from Egypt.*

¹⁷ *I've perfumed my bed with myrrh, aloes, and cinnamon.*

¹⁸ *Come, let's drink our fill of love until morning. Let's enjoy each other's caresses,*

¹⁹ *for my husband is not home. He's away on a long trip.*

²⁰ *He has taken a wallet full of money with him, and he won't return until later in the month."*

²¹ *So she seduced him with her pretty speech. With her flattery she enticed him.*

²² *He followed her at once, like an ox going to the slaughter or like a trapped stag,*

²³ *awaiting the arrow that would pierce its heart. He was like a bird flying into a snare, little knowing it would cost him his life.*

²⁴ *Listen to me, my sons, and pay attention to my words.*

²⁵ *Don't let your hearts stray away toward her. Don't wander down her wayward path.*

²⁶ *For she has been the ruin of many; numerous men have been her victims.*

²⁷ *Her house is the road to the grave. Her bedroom is the den of death.*

3. Based upon Proverbs 7, circle the correct answer to the following questions, and record which verse (or verses) caused you to choose that answer:

    a. Does the Immoral Woman plan her sin; is it premeditated?

        Yes   No   verse(s)_____

    b. Is the Immoral Woman's behavior a one-time event, or is she a serial adulteress?

        One-time event   Serial adulteress   verse(s)_____

    c. Is the Immoral Woman religious?

        Yes   No   verse(s)_____

Proverbs 7:10 tells us that the Immoral Woman dresses "seductively" which means she dresses with the intent to entice her prey. Her body is her bait, and she makes sure her clothes leave very little to a man's imagination.

Today, many women are dressing just like the Immoral Woman…and sadly, some of them are Christians. Nancy Leigh DeMoss, a Christian author and teacher (www.reviveourhearts.com), has a wonderful message entitled *Does God Really Care What I Wear?* I love the question in that title. Let's find the answer together right now.

4. Read 1 Timothy 2:9–10 and 1 Peter 3:3–4 and record what you learn about God's dress code for women.

5. Based upon what you've learned today from Proverbs 7 and 1 Peter 3, please answer the following questions:

    a. Should the speech, dress, attitude or lifestyle of a Christian woman resemble the Immoral Woman's in any way?

        Yes   No

    b. Does God care what we wear?

        Yes   No

    c. Do you think it's possible to dress in a stylish, fashionable way and remain within God's dress code?

        Yes   No

6. What insights has the Lord revealed to you today, and what does He want you to do with them?

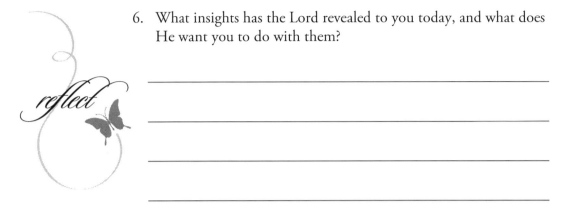

_____

_____

_____

_____

NOTE: Another excellent online source that addresses the subject of modesty and Christian dress is an article entitled *Modesty Heart Check.* It includes some fantastic guidelines to help women make godly decisions regarding their dress. You really need to check it out—especially if you have a daughter. To read this fantastic article visit **www.girltalkhome.com/blog/modesty_heart_check2/**. Many of the April 2006 entries deal with the subject of modesty and fashion as well, and I highly recommend that you read and share them with others.

• • • • •

DAY THREE

1. As you can see by today's Proverb, the old "ignorance is bliss" philosophy is a lie. In fact, Jesus said, "You shall know the truth, and the truth shall make you free" (John 8:32 *NAS*). Spend a few moments in prayer thanking God for the wisdom, knowledge, and truth He's given you through His liberating, life-changing Word.

> *Wisdom will enter your heart,*
> *and knowledge will fill you with joy.*
> —Proverbs 2:10

This Bible study has been percolating in my heart for well over a year. It started as I was preparing a message for a women's event at my church. My text was Proverbs, and while I was studying I saw something that stunned me. You saw it yesterday when you studied Proverbs 7, the lengthy passage describing the Immoral Woman.

Specifically, the verse that shocked me was Proverbs 7:14. It's where the Immoral Woman says, "I've offered my sacrifices and just finished my vows." I'd seen that verse before, but until then I'd never noticed the dark reality it reveals: the Immoral Woman is a religious, churchgoing woman.

Don't get me wrong. I'm not saying the Immoral Woman is a Christian. I don't believe she is. But here's what I do know: she does attend church, and she is religious. And based upon Proverbs 7:15 (where she says, "It's you I was looking for!"), I believe she goes to church to hunt for her next victim.

How does all of this apply to you and me? First of all, we need to be cautious in our relationships (even in our church relationships) because the Immoral Woman has the ability to deceive men and women alike. She may even want to be your best buddy, so beware.

Secondly, warn your husband, son, or daughter if you see a woman fitting her description initiating a relationship with them—even at church. Thirdly, examine your own heart and habits. Are you consciously or unconsciously imitating the Immoral Woman's behavior in your interactions and relationships with men—even, perhaps, with men in your church?

Today we'll take a deeper look at the topic of immorality by studying several New Testament passages. But right now, before you even pick up your Bible and start to study, will you commit to conform your heart and life to what you're about to learn?

2. Where does immorality begin? Read Matthew 15:19 and record the answer to this question.

3. Read 1 Corinthians 6:9–20 and answer these questions:

   a. What do verses 9–11 teach about the Christian and immorality?

   b. According to verses 13–18, why is sexual immorality more serious and detrimental than other types of sin?

   c. What clear instruction is given regarding sexual immorality in verse 18?

   d. According to verses 19–20, who owns the "rights" to your body, and what is your responsibility regarding your body?

4. In today's culture, sexual temptation is everywhere. We're all challenged and tempted on a daily basis by immorality of one form or another. Temptation itself is not a sin, but giving in to the temptation is.

Listed below are several very common ways we experience sexual temptation. Check each box that represents an area of temptation for you, and complete the sentence by describing a practical way you can flee immorality.

❑ Immoral thoughts and fantasies: I can flee this temptation by _____

_____

❑ Immoral television programs: I can flee this temptation by _____

_____

_____

❑ Immoral internet sites and ads: I can flee this temptation by _____

_____

❑ Immoral reading material (magazines and books): I can flee this temptation by

_____

❑ Immoral movies: I can flee this temptation by _____

_____

❑ Men (other than your husband) who are flirtatious and/or sexually suggestive in their behavior: I can flee this temptation by _____

_____

❑ Women whose conversation or behavior is sexually suggestive or explicit: I can flee this temptation by _____

_____

Before you study your final passage for the day, I want to recommend a great resource to you. Covenant Eyes (www.covenanteyes.com) is an internet integrity and accountability program. It monitors every website your computer visits and sends periodic emailed reports of each site visited to an accountability partner of your choice. It's a great way to help you, your family members, or friends to "flee immorality." Check it out!

5. Read 1 Thessalonians 4:3–7 and answer the following questions:

   a. What does God instruct us to control and how (verse 4)?

   b. According to verse 6, what are the repercussions of sexual immorality?

   c. What is God's standard for the way we live (verse 7)?

6. As a result of what you've studied today, what primary principle has God revealed to you?

reflect

_____

_____

_____

_____

_____

DAY FOUR

1. God is so proud of you! You're taking time today to give Him and His Word priority. And it will make such a difference in your life. I trust you're already seeing the blessings of seeking Him first. Spend a few moments in prayer, thanking Him for enriching your life with His love, wisdom, and guidance.

> *(Wisdom) offers you life in her right hand,*
> *and riches and honor in her left.*
> *She will guide you down delightful paths;*
> *all her ways are satisfying.*
> —Proverbs 3:16–17

    Flirting, flattering, and flaunting it. You know who that describes. That's exactly how the Immoral Woman operates and attracts men. So what about the biblically beautiful woman? How can she attract a man—and not just a man, but the right kind of man?

    Today we'll be studying a positive role model from the Old Testament. Her name is Ruth, and she'll teach us the right way to attract Mr. Right.

2. Read Ruth 1–3. As you read, keep a close eye on Ruth. Examine and analyze her carefully. As you pick up on various aspects of her character and behavior, record your observations on the chart on the next page. **NOTE: If you are doing this study with a group, record the chapter and verses related to your observations. This will be very helpful during your small group discussion.**

The Character and Behavior of Ruth: The Right Way to Attract Mr. Right

<u>Chapter 1</u>

<u>Chapter 2</u>

<u>Chapter 3</u>

NOTE: Verses 7–9 must be interpreted in the light of the manners and customs of the Old Testament. By lying at his feet and requesting Boaz to cover her with his garment, Ruth was symbolically asking him to protect her and become her kinsman redeemer. As the kinsman of her deceased husband and father-in-law (Ruth 1:2–5, 2:1, 20), Boaz could legally purchase (redeem) their property from Naomi (Ruth 4:3–5) and acquire Ruth as his wife.

3. Based upon what you have learned about Ruth, how would you counsel another woman (or your daughter) to find Mr. Right? Or if you have a son, what counsel would you give him about finding Mrs. Right?

4. Ruth 4 records the happy ending to the story of Ruth and Boaz. Take a few minutes to read it. It is so beautiful.

5. What characteristic in Ruth's life do you most desire in yours? Explain your answer.

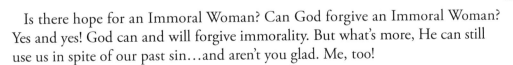

_____

_____

_____

_____

* * * * *

DAY FIVE

1. Reach out to God today through prayer, embracing Him and the wisdom He's given you this week.

> *Wisdom is a tree of life to those who embrace her;*
> *happy are those who hold her tightly.*
> —Proverbs 3:18

Is there hope for an Immoral Woman? Can God forgive an Immoral Woman? Yes and yes! God can and will forgive immorality. But what's more, He can still use us in spite of our past sin…and aren't you glad. Me, too!

If you're struggling with past sin and immorality, may today's study encourage your heart, renew your hope, and reignite your joy.

2. Matthew 1 records the genealogy of Jesus. Read Matthew 1:3–6, then record the female name(s) (mothers) mentioned in the blanks below.

Matthew 1:3–6 *(NLT)*

³ *Judah was the father of Perez and Zerah (whose mother was Tamar). Perez was the father of Hezron. Hezron was the father of Ram.*

⁴ *Ram was the father of Amminadab. Amminadab was the father of Nahshon. Nahshon was the father of Salmon.*

⁵ *Salmon was the father of Boaz (whose mother was Rahab). Boaz was the father of Obed (whose mother was Ruth). Obed was the father of Jesse.*

⁶ *Jesse was the father of King David. David was the father of Solomon (whose mother was Bathsheba, the widow of Uriah).*

Matthew 1:3 _____

Matthew 1:5 _____ and _____

Matthew 1:6 _____

Each of these women has something in common: immorality. One disguised herself and seduced her father-in-law (Genesis 38:13–18). Another was a prostitute (Joshua 2:1). One was raised in a city where her family participated in an idolatrous, immoral form of religion (Ruth 1:15). The other committed adultery (2 Samuel 11:2–5).

Yet here they are, included in the genealogy of Jesus. Amazing grace, indeed!

3. As you read Matthew 1:1–6, did you notice that one of the women listed was related to someone we studied yesterday? Take another look at Matthew 1:5a, and fill in the blanks below:

_____ was the mother of _____,

4. Let's look a little more carefully at Rahab. We need to understand why God forgave and blessed her in such a beautiful way. Read the following passages, and record what you learn about Rahab and how she came to faith in God:

   a. Joshua 2:1–14

   b. Joshua 6:22–25

   c. Hebrews 11:31

   d. James 2:25–26

   Another evidence of Rahab's faith and changed life is Boaz, her son. As you read the Book of Ruth yesterday, you must have noticed Boaz's godly character. I believe his mother's faith influenced his own. God blessed and forgave a former Immoral Woman, gave her a godly son, and included them both in the lineage of His own Son. I don't know about you, but I need to take timeout for a glory shout. Join me, won't you? Glory to God!

5. Let's look at one final passage today. Read John 8:3–11, and answer the following questions:

   a. How is the woman in this passage described (verse 3)?

   b. What was Jesus' response and instruction to the woman (verses 10–11)?

   c. What is Jesus teaching us in this passage?

6. As you conclude this second week of study, take a few minutes to journal what the Lord has done in your heart by completing the following sentence:

My Journal

This week the Lord...

_____

_____

_____

_____

_____

I learned how to study the Bible from a former Immoral Woman. Kay Arthur, author, Bible teacher, and co-founder of Precept Ministries, is that woman. And I'm only one of the thousands upon thousands of lives God has enabled Kay to reach and teach.

Many years ago, when she was a young wife and mother, Kay divorced her husband. Soon after that, she spiraled into an immoral, promiscuous lifestyle. She was desperately searching for love, but all she found was sorrow—until she met Jesus. After that, everything about her changed. The Lord even changed Kay's heart toward her husband, and she decided to return to him. But before she could, he committed suicide.

As a single mother, Kay hungered for God and began devouring His Word. She grew "in the grace and knowledge of the Lord" (2 Peter 3:18). She became a godly woman—a biblically beautiful woman. And eventually, God led Kay to her "Boaz," Jack Arthur.

Several years after they married, Kay and Jack founded Precept Ministries, and God has blessed, multiplied and grown it into a worldwide outreach. All over the globe, people have learned how to study God's Word through the Bible studies Kay has written and through the excellent training Precept provides.

My dear sister, don't let your past define your present or prevent you from God's plan for your future. Accept His grace and forgiveness through the blood of His Son. Become the biblically beautiful woman He wants you to be. I'm so grateful Kay Arthur did.

Week Two • THE IMMORAL WOMAN VS. THE GODLY WOMAN

Biblical Beauty Don't: The Immoral Woman:

1) *How does she speak?* Prov. 2:16, 5:3

   _____, flirtatious, flattering, and enticing words.

2) *How does she act?* Prov. 7:10–16

   Aggressive, brash, rebellious, neglects her home, prefers the _____,

   _____, and _____.

3) *How does she dress?* Prov. 7:10

   Seductively, _____, inappropriately.

4) *What is her heart like?* Prov. 5:6, 30:20

   Religious but _____ God's ways.

5) *What is her destiny?* Prov. 5:5

   Destruction, death, and _____.

Biblical Beauty Do: The Godly Woman:

1) *How does she speak?* 1 Peter 3:3–4

   _____, _____, discreet, and edifying words.

2) *How does she act?* 1 Peter 3:2, 1 Thess. 4:3–7

   Avoids sexual _____, controls her body so as not to _____

   others. *Defraud* = *to take advantage of someone; to cause someone to stumble.*

3) *How does she dress?* 1 Timothy 2:9–10

   _____, decently, and _____.

4) *What is her heart like?* 1 Thess. 4:1

   Longs to _____ God and lead a holy life.

5) *What is her destiny?* 1 Thess. 5:9–10

   _____ _____ and salvation.

Week Three • THE INDISCREET WOMAN

Granmuhver. It's my new favorite word. It took Ezra, my grandson, almost two years to be able to say it. "Nana" or "Mimi" would have been much easier for him to master, but I come from a long line of "Grandmothers," so that particular title was dear to me. For months and months, Ezra struggled with the formidable three-syllable word. But his perseverance paid off this week as "Granmuhver" rolled off his tongue to the cheers of the very one he addressed.

I think one of the reasons God gives us grandchildren is to give us a second chance to learn what we somehow failed to learn with our own children. Watching Ezra struggle to learn my name has given me a new understanding of God's patience with me.

Back in my twenties and thirties, I spent way too much time beating myself up for my failures and lack of spiritual progress. And at times I thought God was even more put out with me than I was. But as a grandmother, I now see what God likely saw back then. He saw me striving and persevering to grow and mature as a Christian, but He also saw there were many formidable three-syllable disciplines that I couldn't master yet...so He patiently waited as I grew.

God's patience. Our perseverance. These are the principles I want to plant in your heart as we begin this week's lesson on the topic of "discretion"—another formidable three-syllable word. It cannot be attained overnight, but as we persevere and God patiently watches, we can become biblically beautiful women of discretion. Sister, let's persevere 'til we hear God's cheer.

Well done, my good and faithful servant.
—Matthew 25:21

DAY ONE

1. As you can see by today's Proverb, Wisdom's friends are
   Prudence, Knowledge, and Discretion. Pray, asking God to
   show you how to make them your friends, too.

> *"I, wisdom, dwell together with prudence;*
> *I possess knowledge and discretion."*
> —Proverbs 8:12 *NIV*

Allow me to re-introduce you to our Beauty Don't #2, the **Indiscreet Woman**.
Unlike the Immoral Woman, who is given so much space in the Proverbs, the
Indiscreet Woman is only mentioned once. But that single verse packs a real
punch. You read it in Week One, but just in case you've forgotten, here it is:

> *A woman who is beautiful but lacks discretion*
> *is like a gold ring in a pig's snout.*
> —Proverbs 11:22

It's kind of funny at first (can't you just picture a proud pig wearing a pretty
gold ring), but that passage isn't just intended to amuse. This proverbial
put-down also contains a powerful message about the necessity of discretion.

There may only be one verse dedicated to the Indiscreet Woman, but there are
plenty of verses in Proverbs that instruct and exhort us to obtain discretion and
prudence. Today you'll discover why you need both.

2. You recorded definitions for the words "discretion," "discreet," "indiscreet,"
   and "prudent" in Day Two of your Week One homework (page 7). Take a few
   moments to briefly revisit and review those definitions.

In Proverbs 11:22, the word "discretion" means "taste, judgment, and
discernment."[1] It can also mean "mental or spiritual perception or discernment."[2]
This means the beautiful woman in Proverbs 11:22 had poor taste, bad
judgment, no discernment, and lacked mental or spiritual perception—a recipe
for a disastrous life. Can you see why discretion is so necessary? Without it,
you're actually setting yourself up for the perfect storm to strike and destroy you.

3. Read each passage on the following chart, and record what you learn about
   the benefits of discretion and the specific ways it can protect you:

The Benefits of Discretion

NOTE: **Depending on your Bible translation, the word "discretion" may be translated as wise/wisdom, prudent, discernment, or sensible.**

Proverbs 2:11–17—*Discretion will…*
Proverbs 3:21–26—*Discretion will…*
Proverbs 19:11—*Discretion will…*

4. You have just seen the benefits of discretion. But what does discretion look like? How does a woman of discretion behave? And most importantly, how can you know whether or not you possess discretion? The answers to these questions are found in Proverbs as Solomon contrasts the behavior of the discreet and prudent with the foolish and simple.

    Read the following verses from Proverbs noting what you learn about the behavior of the discreet versus the behavior of the fool. Keep in mind that prudence, wisdom, and knowledge are synonyms of discretion. To give you a head start, I've completed the first one for you.

NOTE: To enhance your understanding, read each verse from two or three Bible translations. One of the simplest ways to access a variety of translations is by visiting www.biblegateway.com. It will also make completing the chart much easier.

Read:	A discreet/prudent person…	But a fool/simple person…
Prov. 12:16	*overlooks or remains calm when insulted*	*gets angry fast*
Prov. 13:16		
Prov. 14:15		
Prov. 14:18		
Prov. 15:5		
Prov. 22:3		

5. Ask God to show you one or two specific areas in your life where you need to develop discretion and prudence. Record your insights.

_____

_____

_____

_____

· · · · ·

DAY TWO

1. You have influence. Whether it's with your friends, family, or fellow workers, your life influences others. Are you advising them wisely? Are you helping them succeed? Your responsibility as a woman of influence is huge. Get on your knees right now and ask God to give you wisdom in your relationships, conversations and dealings with others.

> *"Good advice and success belong to me (wisdom)*
> *Insight and strength are mine.*
> *Because of me, kings reign, and rulers make just laws.*
> *Rulers lead with my help, and nobles make righteous judgments."*
> —Proverbs 8:14–16

We spent yesterday entirely in Proverbs, but today we are going to get out and meet one of the most fascinating women in the Bible. Her name is Abigail, and she's a role model of discretion, prudence and wisdom. I think you're going to love her. She's certainly taught me a lot—can't wait to meet her one day! Enjoy your time today with Abigail.

2. Pick up your Bible and get to know Abigail by reading 1 Samuel 25:1–42, then record your insights to the following questions:

a. What kind of woman is Abigail? How is she described?

b. What is her husband like, and how would his behavior likely have affected Abigail on a day-to-day basis?

c. What choice did Abigail make when her servant informed her (verses 14–17) of Nabal's decision? Do you think she made the right decision and, if so, why?

d. How did Abigail's actions and speech reveal her discretion, prudence, and wisdom?

e. What immediate and future benefits did Abigail receive because of her discretion and prudence?

3. You've seen how wisely Abigail handled her foolish husband and the life and death situation she and her loved ones faced. Now I want you to think about another very different scenario: what if Abigail had been an Indiscreet Woman? Ponder that for a moment, and record your answers to the following questions:

   a. What choices might an Indiscreet Woman (a woman lacking wisdom and knowledge) have made when faced with the dire situation Nabal created, and what possible repercussions would have followed?

   b. If Abigail had been an Indiscreet Woman, how might David's future have been affected (verses 30–34, 39)?

4. We all have to deal with foolish, difficult people at times. What insights did you learn from Abigail to help you deal with the Nabal's in your life?

   _____

   _____

   _____

   _____

DAY THREE

1. As you read today's Proverb, I hope you are encouraged by God's invitation to freely give you wisdom. Take Him up on His offer. Ask Him to give you wisdom as you study His Word today.

   Listen as Wisdom calls out! Hear as understanding raises her voice!
   ... At the entrance to the city, at the city gates, she cries aloud,
   "I call to you, to all of you! I am raising my voice to all people.
   How naïve you are! Let me give you some common sense.
   O foolish ones, let me give you understanding."
   —Proverbs 8:1–5

   "Discretion" used to be one of those innocuous, vanilla-sounding words that I associated with…well, "boring." I knew it was closely related to the word "prudent" (another unpopular, seldom-used word) but to be honest, both words were a little yawn-inducing to me. Not anymore.

   God's Word has completely changed the negative connotations I used to associate with the words "discretion" and "prudence." Although I don't often use those specific words (and I'm guessing you probably don't either), I do use positive terms like "smart," "discerning," "spiritually sharp," and "wise" to describe discreet, prudent people.

   Whatever you may choose to call them, discretion and prudence are keys that can unlock your God-given potential. My goal today is to take you into God's Word where He can whet your appetite to live up to that potential. My prayer is that you will take what He teaches you and run with it.

2. Yesterday, when you studied Abigail, you also met David. Today, we'll go back to an earlier period of David's life when he was a young shepherd living at home with his family. Read 1 Samuel 16:14–22 and answer the following questions:

   a. In this passage, you learned that David was a skillful musician, but what did you learn about his character (verse 18)?

b. What was the result of David's discretion and prudence (verses 19–22)?

c. As stated earlier, David was very young when he began serving King Saul. What does this fact reveal about discretion, prudence, wisdom, and discernment? Before you answer this question, read Proverbs 20:11 for additional insight.

3. Joseph, another Old Testament character, was a young man whose jealous brothers sold him to slave traders who, in turn, took him to Egypt. While he was there, Joseph was wrongly convicted and jailed. But because of his God-given ability to interpret dreams, he was eventually summoned to appear before Pharaoh to interpret Pharaoh's dream. Read Genesis 41:25–49 and answer the following questions:

a. What was the result of Joseph's discretion, discernment, and wisdom (verses 38–49)?

b. Pharaoh (a man who did not worship God) recognized Joseph's discretion, discernment, and wisdom. What does this reveal?

c. How old was Joseph when he interpreted Pharaoh's dream (verse 46), and what does that reveal about wisdom, discretion, and discernment?

4. Whether you consider yourself young, old, or somewhere in the middle, what insights have you learned today to apply to your own life? How are you doing when it comes to discretion?

reflect

_____

_____

_____

_____

_____

• • • • •

DAY FOUR

1. One of the things I love the most about the incredibly prudent group of Old Testament characters we have studied over the past two days is their humility. Humble yourself before the Lord today in prayer, and ask Him to help you stay that way.

pray

> *Don't be impressed with your own wisdom.*
> *Instead, fear the Lord and turn away from evil.*
> —Proverbs 3:7

In your study of Abigail, David, and Joseph, you have seen real-life examples of what discretion looks like. You have also seen the powerful way God can use those who possess it. Today you will meet another incredible Old Testament character.

Daniel. It is my heartfelt prayer that God will use Abigail, David, Joseph, and Daniel to inspire and encourage you to become a modern-day example of discretion before your family, friends, neighbors, and co-workers. May all who know and encounter you witness the biblical beauty mark of discretion upon your life.

2. Daniel was a young Jewish man who was taken into Babylonian captivity where he served King Nebuchadnezzar. One night, the king had a dream, and none of his magicians or wise men could interpret it. As a result, Nebuchadnezzar ordered their deaths and the deaths of Daniel and his friends. Read the following passages and questions, and record what you learn:

   a. Daniel 2:12–19—What did you learn about Daniel's character (verses 14, 16–19)?

   b. Daniel 2:46–48—What was the result of Daniel's wisdom, discretion, and prudence?

3. Joseph, David, Abigail, and Daniel all shared: 1) a common faith in God, and 2) the attributes of discretion, prudence, discernment, and wisdom. But there's something else they shared in common, and here's a hint: what happened to each of them after their discretion and prudence was recognized by others?

4. When it comes to the workplace:

    a. How can a deficit of discretion affect someone's professional life?

    b. What are the potential professional benefits of possessing discretion?

    I hate to bring it up, but you and I both know that a lack of discretion doesn't just affect our family and business relationships. Indiscretion can destroy even the best of friendships. And let's just call it what it really is: gabbing and gossiping. We've both been guilty of it, and we've both been hurt by it. Our final study today will remind us of the dangers of indiscretion and the blessings of just keeping our mouths shut.

5. Read the following scriptures, and record what you learn about the dangers of indiscretion, the blessings of discretion, and how to preserve precious friendships:

    a. Proverbs 11:13

    b. Proverbs 16:28

c. Proverbs 17:9

d. Proverbs 17:28

e. Proverbs 21:23

6. As you reflect upon your own personal and professional relationships, how and with whom are you most challenged to be discreet? What specific, scriptural steps can you take to become a woman of discretion?

_____

_____

_____

_____

• • • • •

DAY FIVE

1. Everyone wants to have joy, and those who follow wisdom usually do. Take a few minutes to praise and thank God for the joy He has brought you, and for the sorrow He has saved you from all because of the wisdom He has given you.

"My children, listen to me (wisdom), for all who follow my ways are joyful. ...Joyful are those who listen to me, watching for me daily at my gates, waiting for me outside my home."

—Proverbs 8:32–34

Discretion and prudence are in short supply in today's world. Are you ready to begin making up for that deficit? You can. God has given you everything you need to become a woman of influence and discretion. And as you have seen in your homework this week, one discreet woman can make a huge difference in so many lives. May your study today encourage you to step up and be that woman.

2. Prudence and discretion are synonymous with wisdom, and one of the most encouraging passages about wisdom is found in 1 Corinthians. Please read 1 Corinthians 1:18–2:16 circling the words "wise" and "wisdom" each time you see them. Record what you learn about wisdom by answering the following questions:

   a. Two kinds of wisdom are contrasted in 1 Corinthians. What are they (verses 1:21, 24, 30, 2:5–8)?

   b. Who can attain God's wisdom and how (verses 24–30)?

   c. According to 1 Corinthians 2:12 and 2:16, what else has God given us and why?

   d. How did this passage encourage you as you seek to become a woman of wisdom and discretion?

3. You have just seen what God has done to give you discretion, prudence, wisdom, and discernment. But I want you to focus on two other areas in your life that will greatly determine your ability to grow in wisdom and discretion. Read the following verses and record what you learn:

a. Proverbs 13:20

b. Hebrews 5:12–14, 1 Peter 2:2

4. How can you be an example of discretion and prudence to others and especially to unbelievers? Read Colossians 4:5–6, your final passage for the week, and record what you learn.

Guess what? We're halfway through our study of biblical beauty. Thank you for your dedication and commitment!

My favorite Old Testament verse says, "And He humbled you and let you be hungry, and fed you with manna which you did not know, nor did your fathers know, that He might make you understand that man does not live by bread alone, but man lives by everything that proceeds out of the mouth of the Lord" (Deuteronomy 8:3 NASB). I'm praying you're feeling really full right now because of the feast God has fed you over the past three weeks. God bless you for giving His Word priority!

5. Spend a few minutes journaling what the Lord has done in your heart this week through His Word by completing the following sentence:

My Journal

This week the Lord...

_____

_____

_____

_____

I was having a very difficult time with a very difficult person. Nothing I could say or do seemed to improve the relationship, and I could not understand why. It was a puzzle I could not solve. What I needed was a great, big, heaping dose of discretion—but I didn't know that. Thank God, He did. And He knew just the woman who could give it to me.

One evening while I was at a friend's house, I picked up a book she had by an author I had heard of but had never read before. As I perused through its pages, I was astonished; it described my difficult relationship in detail. I borrowed that book, took it straight home, and read it all night. And somewhere in the wee hours of the morning, God used the words of that author to give me the wisdom I needed to deal with that relationship the right way. The prudent way. The discreet way.

Since that time, I have read almost every book Jan Silvious has written. A gifted author, speaker, and Christian counselor, Jan is also an amazing woman of discretion and discernment. I am serious when I tell you that you need to get your hands on every book she has written. Practical, biblical, witty, and intelligent, Jan epitomizes the biblically beautiful attributes of prudence and discretion.

As I've said before, we can't become women of discretion overnight. But spending time with wonderful authors like Jan Silvious can get us there a whole lot faster.

Want to find out more about

Jan Silvious

and her books?

Visit her online at
www.jansilvious.com

Week Three • THE INDISCREET WOMAN VS. THE WOMAN OF DISCRETION

Key Verse: *A woman who is beautiful but lacks discretion is like a gold ring in a pig's snout.*—Proverbs 11:22

OT synonyms for discretion:
discreet, discerning, prudent, understanding, insight, wise, knowledge

NT synonyms for discretion:
discreet, sensible, sober, self-controlled, wisdom

Biblical Beauty Don't:
<u>*The Indiscreet Woman:*</u>

1) She _____ too much and _____ whatever comes into her head.

2) She _____ at personal and _____ growth.

3) She makes _____ _____ based on bad judgment.

4) She's _____ and enjoys _____.

5) She _____ with danger and _____ it.

Biblical Beauty Do:
<u>*The Discreet Woman:*</u>

1) She _____ her _____ and speaks with wisdom. *Prov. 10:13, 11:12*

2) She's eager to learn, _____, and mature _____. *Prov. 14:6*

3) She makes _____ _____ based on truth. *Prov. 13:16, 14:15*

4) She is _____-_____ and not easily angered. *Prov. 17:27*

5) She _____ danger and _____ it. *Prov. 27:12*

Week Four • THE IRRITATING WOMAN

Wouldn't you know it. Mere seconds before I began writing this lesson on the Beauty Don't #3, the **Irritating Woman**, I opened my mouth and became that woman. I should have seen it coming.

Clue #1: My husband Bill had been doing a small home repair project. Home repair projects seldom go smoothly at the Cole house. This should have alerted me to the very real possibility that things could be heading south fast.

Clue #2 came in the form of a question: "Do we have an X-Acto knife," Bill asked. Scary. So, I took a deep breath and replied, "Yes, it's in the pantry in the tool drawer." But I knew I should also have said, "Let me go get it and bring it to you." But I didn't. I didn't want to. "Let him get it," I thought to myself, "He's a big boy." And that sassy little selfish attitude was Clue #3.

Less than five minutes later, that contentious, crabby Irritating Woman appeared.

I walked into the room where Bill was doing the repair, and to my absolute horror I discovered he wasn't using an X-Acto knife. No, it turned out, he couldn't find the X-Acto knife so he was using one of my very best kitchen knives. That man was carving into drywall with my good knife! Gasping, then erupting, I exploded. Words gushed from my mouth…followed by silence. Too much silence if you know what I mean.

Fortunately, I have a very forgiving husband. After I apologized, peace prevailed. But oh, how I hate it when I foolishly ignore every obvious clue around me and give in to the Irritating Woman.

I wonder. Has the Irritating Woman shown up at your house lately? Have the people at your job ever met her? Are you ready to banish bossy ol' Beauty Don't #3 and replace her with her biblically beautiful counterpart, the Edifying Woman? Well then, this lesson is for you. Oh, who am I kidding. This lesson is for me, too.

DAY ONE

1. The message of today's proverb is obvious. Ask God to take the limp out of your spiritual walk by committing to be led by His wisdom.

> *If you live a life guided by wisdom,*
> *you won't limp or stumble as you run.*
> —Proverbs 4:12 *NLT*

The Irritating Woman is mentioned five times in Proverbs, and each time it says practically the same thing. So I ask, wouldn't one mention have been enough? I mean, after the second and third reference to such a shrewish, contentious woman, it really threatens to give us girls a bad rap.

But God loves us, girl—and He "gets" us, too. And He repeats His message about the Irritating Woman because He desires the very best for us. Hold that thought as we begin our study of Beauty Don't #3.

2. Read each of the five verses about the Irritating Woman, and answer the questions that follow.

> *A nagging wife annoys like a constant dripping.*
> —Proverbs 19:13

> *It is better to live alone in the corner of an attic*
> *than with a contentious wife in a lovely home.*
> —Proverbs 21:9

> *It is better to live alone in the desert*
> *than with a crabby, complaining wife.*
> —Proverbs 21:19

> *It is better to live alone in the corner of an attic*
> *than with a quarrelsome wife in a lovely home.*
> —Proverbs 25:24

> *A quarrelsome wife is as annoying as*
> *a constant dripping on a rainy day.*
> *Stopping her complaints is like trying to stop the wind*
> *or trying to hold something with greased hands.*
> —Proverbs 27:15–16

Beauty by THE BOOK

a. How is the Irritating Woman described? Answer this question by circling the specific adjectives used to describe her.

b. Now let's broaden our perspective about the Irritating Woman. What are some synonyms for the words you just circled? What do you call a woman like this (careful!)? Feel free to use a Thesaurus if you need help (www.Thesaurus.com is a great resource, but be even more careful). Record several synonyms.

c. As you look at the words you circled and the synonyms you found, it is easy to see the downside of being married to an Irritating Woman. In fact, three of the five verses begin with the same six words, and they describe exactly how her husband feels. Record those words in the blanks below along with your thoughts about what a husband like that might do.

_____ _____ _____ _____ _____ _____ _____

3. By now you have a pretty clear picture of the Irritating Woman and the effect she has upon her husband and those who live with her. But what kind of effect does she have upon her friends, co-workers, and those who cross her path on a regular basis? Draw upon your own recent run-ins with the Irritating Woman to complete the following sentences:

a. *Just being around an Irritating Woman makes me* _____

_____

b. *One Irritating Woman in a group or family setting can* _____

_____

4. Your answers thus far reveal the negative impact the Irritating Woman has upon others. But what about her? Does her contentious behavior cost her anything? Read the following verses, and record what you learn about the consequences of being an Irritating Woman:

   a. Proverbs 13:3

   b. Proverbs 18:6–7

   c. Proverbs 18:19

5. One example of the dangerous consequences of becoming an Irritating Woman (especially if you're married) is found in 2 Samuel 6:12–23. It details an encounter between David and his wife Michal. Read this passage, picturing it in your mind as you read, and answer the following questions:

   a. What had David done that provoked Michal, and what does this reveal about her?

   b. Before Michal ever said a word to David, what had she already done (verse 16)?

c. Note how the conversation between Michal and David began (verse 20). Who started it, and what does this tell you?

d. How would you describe Michal's words to David?

e. What consequences did Michal experience in her life and marriage as a result of her words and attitude (verse 23)?

6. As you reflect upon what you've learned today, why do you think the Irritating Woman is repeated five times in the Proverbs?

_____

_____

_____

_____

· · · · ·

DAY TWO

1. The Irritating Woman seems to bring out the worst in others. Her crabbiness and contentiousness pushes everybody's buttons. So what can you do to prevent being sucked in? To answer that question, read today's proverb. Then pray and ask God to protect you the next time an Irritating Woman starts to get on your last nerve.

> *Wisdom will save you from evil people,*
> *from those whose speech is corrupt.*
> —Proverbs 2:12

Yesterday, you saw the dangers and consequences of becoming an Irritating Woman. She annoys and aggravates others; she offends her friends; and she undermines and destroys her own marriage. Anyone can see the fallout of her flawed behavior. A path of destruction follows her everywhere she goes. And if she refuses to change, her life will devolve into a series of broken relationships and a resumé littered with a long line of previous employers.

If the downside of becoming an Irritating Woman is so obvious, then why do we struggle so hard with becoming just like her? That's the first question we'll address in today's homework, but there's another and Dr. Phil might pose it like this: "What's the payoff for an Irritating Woman?" Another way to phrase it might be, "What motivates us to irritate others?"

If it sounds like today's study involves a little therapy, you're right. But relax. You won't have to lie down on a couch or be analyzed by anyone who bears any resemblance to Dr. Phil. All you have to do is read your Bible and ask God to search your heart through the power of His Spirit.

But be prepared. The Holy Spirit won't always tell you what you want to hear. He'll never justify contentious, crabby behavior; and your tired excuses won't work with Him: "But Lord, I'm only like that once a month," or, "But somebody's got to run this house, Lord" or, "You know I can't help it, God, I'm just so outspoken." Any of these sound familiar?

One more thing: the Holy Spirit's diagnosis is always accurate, but unlike Dr. Phil, whatever the Spirit diagnoses, He can also cure. Glory! So pick up your Bible, invite God's Spirit to speak, and let the healing begin.

2. Where did the Irritating Woman come from? Uncovering and understanding her past (and ours) is the logical first step in the therapeutic process which will ultimately lead us to the road to recovery. Genesis 3 records the fall of man (the sin of Adam and Eve) and the resulting consequences. Read God's words to Eve from the translations provided, and answer the questions that follow:

> To the woman He said, "I will greatly multiply Your pain in childbirth,
> In pain you will bring forth children; Yet your desire will be for your husband,
> And he will rule over you."
> —Genesis 3:16 *(NASB95)*

> Then he said to the woman, "I will sharpen the pain of your pregnancy,
> and in pain you will give birth. And you will desire to control your husband,
> but he will rule over you."
> —Genesis 3:16 *(NLT)*

a. How did the fall (sin) change the dynamics of Eve's relationship with Adam?

b. Whether you're married or not, as a descendant of Eve, describe your own struggle with the effects of the fall.

c. Excluding the effects of the fall, who has God clearly called to be the final authority of the home, and why is that often such a challenge for us?

Genesis not only reveals the source and root problem of the Irritating Woman (sin and a desire to control), it opens the door to another topic that is a sore subject with some women: submission. The Bible clearly teaches that women are to submit to their own husbands (not to every man, but to their own husbands), and that husbands are to love their wives as Christ loved the church (Ephesians 5:22-33). Submission basically means that women are to respectfully place themselves under the authority of their husbands.

The scriptural principles of submission do not imply that women are inferior to men. On the contrary, Scripture emphasizes the equality of men and women: "God created man in His own image, in the image of God He created him; male and female He created them" (Genesis 1:27 *NASB*). But even before the fall of man, Adam and Eve had different roles. From the beginning, God created man to lead the home and woman to be his helper (Genesis 2:18). And until the fall, Eve's submission to Adam wasn't a problem; but after the fall, it became a major problem.

Now just in case you're upset (or a little offended) by the concept of submission, please take time to read Philippians 2:5–11. This beautiful passage reveals that Christ—who is equal with God—willingly submitted Himself to God when He came to this earth and died on the cross to save us. In this way, Christ is an example to all of us (men and women alike) of the beauty and importance of submission.

One final thing: submission is not unconditional. A wife is not required to submit to abuse or to ongoing sexual infidelity and immorality. When abuse occurs, a wife should seek protection from civil authorities as well as support from her church. When there is infidelity or immorality, a wife should seek sound, biblical Christian counsel.

Wives aren't the only ones who struggle with the desire to control and the contentious, complaining attitude that this desire breeds. Every woman struggles with it, even spiritually mature women, and you are about to meet one of them.

3. Miriam was the older sister of Moses and Aaron. These three siblings were leaders over the Israelites, but God gave Moses the primary role of authority and leadership. On the greatest day in Israel's history (when God delivered them from Egypt by allowing them to cross the Red Sea on dry ground), God used Miriam in a beautiful way. Read Exodus 15:19–21, and record what you learn about Miriam, her position, and how God used her.

4. Approximately two years after their deliverance from Egypt, another event involving Miriam occurred. Read Numbers 12:1–15, and answer the following questions:

   a. What caused Miriam to become an Irritating Woman (verse 1)? In other words, what set her off?

b. How did Miriam respond (verse 2)?

c. What does Miriam's response reveal about her heart and the real root of her contentious, complaining behavior?

d. What do you think Miriam sought to gain by her quarrelsome complaints? In other words, what payoff was she seeking?

e. What was Miriam's actual payoff (verses 4–15)?

5. Excluding the desire to control others, what else is very often at the root of critical, complaining behavior?

6. Who are the primary earthly authority figures in your life (for example: your husband, boss, supervisor, pastor, teacher, parent, etc.). Write their names in the following blanks, and circle the phrase that best describes your current level of respect and attitude toward them.

	very respectful	mostly respectful	respect varies frequently	mostly disrespectful	very disrespectful
_____	very respectful	mostly respectful	respect varies frequently	mostly disrespectful	very disrespectful
_____	very respectful	mostly respectful	respect varies frequently	mostly disrespectful	very disrespectful
_____	very respectful	mostly respectful	respect varies frequently	mostly disrespectful	very disrespectful
_____	very respectful	mostly respectful	respect varies frequently	mostly disrespectful	very disrespectful
_____	very respectful	mostly respectful	respect varies frequently	mostly disrespectful	very disrespectful
_____	very respectful	mostly respectful	respect varies frequently	mostly disrespectful	very disrespectful

7. How has the Holy Spirit diagnosed the condition of your heart today?

_____

_____

_____

_____

reflect

DAY THREE

1. Wisdom wants to be your sister and best friend, and you could have none better. Ask God to help you get to know Wisdom well so that your friendship with her will flourish and bear much fruit.

> *Say to wisdom, "You are my sister,"*
> *and call insight your intimate friend.*
> —Proverbs 7:4 *RSV*

I don't know about you, but I'm worn out from spending the past two days with irritating women. First there was Michal who taught us how to lose a good husband. Then there was Miriam, who taught us how to rile God's anger through jealousy, envy, and a critical, complaining spirit. Today I had planned for us to study Delilah, another Irritating Woman who could teach us how to nag a strong man weak. But I need a break…and I'm thinking maybe you do, too.

So, let's hang out today with some cool-headed chicks you may not have met before: Mahlah, Noah, Hoglah, Milcah and Tirzah, also known as "the daughters of Zelophehad." These gals really know how to handle themselves. And the beautiful thing about them is this: They know how to get what they want without crabbing, complaining, or even nagging. By the time you've finished reading about them, you may want to name one of your daughters after them—probably not "Hoglah" though!

Enjoy your time with the five biblically beautiful daughters of Zelophehad.

2. Your assignment is simple. Read the following passages, and record your answers to the questions on the chart.

- Numbers 26:33

- Numbers 27:1–10: their meeting with Moses before Israel enters the Promised Land.

- Numbers 36:1–12

- Joshua 17:3–4: their meeting with Joshua after Israel enters the Promised Land.

The Daughters of Zelophehad	
What problems and complications did they face?	How did they handle their problems, and what characteristics did they display?
How would an Irritating Woman handle problems like these?	How would others ultimately benefit from the way they handled their problem?

3. What did you think about the daughters of Zelophehad, and what did the Holy Spirit teach you through their example?

reflect

_____

_____

_____

_____

_____

• • • • •

DAY FOUR

pray

1. Today you will be studying the power of the spoken word. Before you begin, pray and commit to speaking life-giving, refreshing words to every person whose life intersects yours today.

A person's words can be life-giving water;
words of true wisdom are as refreshing as a bubbling brook
—Proverbs 18:4

In Week One, you learned about 3C Syndrome, a malady marked by Contentiousness, Crabbiness and frequent bouts of Complaining—all of the primary symptoms of the Irritating Woman. 3C is easily identified and, as we've learned, all women struggle with it. But men are not immune from it either. Remember Aaron, Moses' brother? He had a pretty bad case of 3C himself.

This week you've discovered:

- The dangers of 3C: destroyed relationships and God's judgment.
- The source of 3C: the sin of your ancestors, Adam and Eve.
- The root causes of 3C: the desire to control others, as well as jealousy, ambition, envy, etc.

Our goal today is to discover the cure for 3C. Yes, hallelujah, there is a cure! It is easily administered, available to everyone, and it can completely reverse the adverse effects of 3C. What is this miraculous remedy? It is something I call 3B. Curious about this cure-all? C'mon, let's get in the Word and get more info.

2. Read Ephesians 4:29.

> *Let no unwholesome word proceed from your mouth,*
> *but only such a word as is good for edification,*
> *according to the need of the moment, that it may give*
> *grace to those who hear.*
>
> —Ephesians 4:29 *NASB*

3. According to Ephesians 4:29, what are the only kind of words you are allowed to speak? Circle the answer in the verse.

Ephesians 4:29 gives us three divine boundaries for every word we speak. First, we must choose words that are "good" (*agathos* in the Greek), which is defined as "benevolent and beneficial."[3] Second, our words must edify (*oikodome* in the Greek), which means to "build up and spiritually profit" others.[4] The final criteria for the words we choose is that they must "give grace" (*charis* in the Greek), which means to bless and benefit others.[5]

In Dr. Spiros Zodhiates' wonderful resource, *The Complete Word Study Dictionary New Testament*, he defines grace like this:

> A favor done without expectation of return; the absolutely free expression of the loving kindness of God to men finding its only motive in the bounty and benevolence of the Giver; unearned and unmerited favor.[6]

What does all of this mean to us? Very simply, it means that the words that flow from our lips must do three things: build, bless, and benefit. This is 3B speech—the cure for 3C. Furthermore, we're to speak these words in way that illustrates and emulates God's grace, which means even if the hearer has not earned and does not deserve to hear 3B words, we must speak them anyway.

Do these boundaries mean we cannot correct, discipline, or honestly express ourselves to others? Absolutely not. But it does mean we must do it in a positive, gracious way with the motivation of building up, not tearing down.

4. Take a few moments to read the verses that follow Ephesians 4:29. Read Ephesians 4:30–32, and answer the following questions:

    a. According to verse 30, what happens when we fail to use 3B speech?

    b. Verse 31 includes several words that are synonymous with 3C speech. What are these synonyms?

    c. 3B speech (an audible expression) begins within our heart. According to verse 32, what kind of heart and attitude produces 3B speech?

    d. According to this passage, will 3B reverse 3C? Circle your answer.

        yes   no

5. What do 3B words look and sound like? To discover practical examples of the specific kinds of words that build, bless and benefit, let's return to Proverbs for a little lesson on "How to Speak 3B." Read each verse on the following chart, and complete the sentence by recording what it teaches about wise, righteous speech. To help you get started, I have completed the first one for you.

How to Speak 3B	
Proverbs 10:11	*3B words... give life to others*
Proverbs 10:21, 12:25	*3B words...*
Proverbs 10:31–32	*3B words...*
Proverbs 15:1	*3B words...*
Proverbs 16:23	*3B words...*

6. Make a list below of the primary people your life touches on a daily basis, then take each name before the Lord in prayer. Ask Him to show you how you can speak 3B to each of them in the specific way they need to hear it. Ask God to give you sensitivity and discernment to their needs. Confess, repent, and commit to turn away from 3C speech and become a woman who only speaks one language: 3B, words that build, bless, and benefit.

7. How has God spoken to your heart today?

_____

_____ *reflect*

_____

_____

DAY FIVE

1. How important is wisdom? Read today's proverb, and commit to seek and apply God's wisdom to your life as though your very life depended on it…because it does.

> *"Whoever finds me (wisdom) finds life and*
> *wins approval from the Lord.*
> *But those who miss me have injured themselves."*
> —Proverbs 8:35–36

I had a reality check at the mall one day. The cell phone of a woman who was shopping just a few feet away from me rang, and she answered it like this, "Where the _____ are you!!" I have no idea how the caller responded, but the woman's loud, profane rant continued for about a minute.

When she hung up, she stashed the phone back into her purse and went right back to her shopping, as though the phone had never rung. I was rattled by the reality of such a public explosion of profanity. But not her. She was less than three feet from me. She knew I had heard her, yet she never said a single "Sorry."

Now let me ask you a question: Who do you think was on the other end of that cell phone? Who do you think that Irritating Woman was talking to? People don't talk to their friends like that, do they? They wouldn't have any friends if they did. I think you and I both know who was on the other end of that cell phone. It was probably a member of that woman's own family, her husband or, perhaps, her child. It still sickens me when I think about that.

Too many people are growing up in homes where words of death are spoken on a daily basis. But we, dear sister, cannot compromise or conform to the common standards of our culture. Our husbands, our children, our friends, and co-workers—even the people who overhear our cell phone conversations—should be the beneficiaries of our grace-filled words.

The principles you will be learning from God's Word today will build on what you learned yesterday about 3B speech. As you embrace and apply these truths to your life, you will not only build, bless, and benefit others, you will become a powerful witness for Christ through your biblically beautiful speech.

2. Attention all wives (and potential wives). God has some very specific instructions for us about our speech and demeanor. Read 1 Peter 3:1–4 and answer the following questions:

    a. What are God's specific instructions to wives who are married to unbelieving husbands? What kind of "words" are they instructed to use. (verses 1–2)

    b. According to verses 3–4, how can a woman be included on God's Best Dressed List (and not be a nominee for Irritating Woman of the Year)?

    The Irritating Woman uses nagging as a way to get others to do what she wants (there's that control issue again). But if we want to be Edifying 3B Women, nagging others has got to go. So, how do we deal with our inner need to nag? A very wise widow taught me a technique about the proper way (and Person) to nag. Let me introduce you to her.

3. Read Luke 18:1–7, and answer the following questions:

    a. What practical principle did you learn from the widow about how to deal with the need to nag?

b. Who are the top two targets of your need to nag? Identify them and take two minutes to practice what you just learned from Luke 18. And the next time you feel the gnawing need to straighten someone out coming over you, think about that widow, and keep practicing her technique.

4. Before you close your Bible and do your weekly journal assignment, there are a few super practical verses I would like for you to look up. These verses contain some great "talking points"—wisdom and instructions to help us in our everyday conversation. Read each verse on the following chart, and briefly record the truth it teaches about talkin'.

Talking Points: Tips For Talkin'	
Proverbs 10:19	
Proverbs 15:23, 25:11	
Proverbs 15:28	
Proverbs 17:14, 20:3	
Proverbs 17:27	

5. What has the Lord taught you this week, and how have you seen Him at work in your life? Journal your thoughts by completing the following sentence:

My Journal

This week the Lord...

_____

_____

_____

_____

_____

More than any other single group of women on the Planet, mother-in-laws rank number one on the Irritating Woman list, and I have officially joined their ranks. It was a role I felt some degree of dread about. I longed for a mother-in-law mentor—until I realized I already had one: my own precious mother-in-law, Frances Cole.

Fran is the model mother-in-law. She's supportive but not smothering. She's interested but not meddlesome. She's strong but not overbearing. And she's sweet, sweet, sweet. Although many miles separate us and our times together are too far and few between, her welcome mat is always out, and her smile outlasts our stay.

Annie Chapman has written a wonderful book for mother-in-laws entitled *The Mother-in-Law Dance*. In one chapter she refers to Proverbs 10:19 (one of the verses we just studied). She says that for mother-in-laws, "Keeping our words to a minimum is one of the smartest ways to stay out of trouble. In fact, most any response that needs to be addressed can be summed up with three individual words. Those words are "sure," "really," and "wow."[7]

When Bill and I were 23 and our first son was a tiny baby, we bought a 40-foot travel trailer and went on the road in evangelism. We traveled from church to church where we sang for revivals and evangelistic meetings. We lived on love offerings, and we trusted God to pay our bills and keep us fed. When I think about what I might do if one of my children did that today, I hope and pray I'd do just what Fran did—say, "Wow," and little else. Fran must have been worried about us...but we never knew it. She kept her concerns to herself—and I'm pretty sure she probably nagged God often on our behalf.

The term "mother-in-law" has historically been associated with adjectives like "aggravating", "troublemaking", "exasperating" and sometimes even "infuriating." But Frances Cole is a biblically beautiful woman who has shattered the stereotypical mother-in-law mold. And these days, I'm working very hard to follow in her footsteps.

Week Four • HOW'S THAT IRRITATING WOMAN WORKING FOR YOU?

The Irritating Woman:

1. Outward signs: _____, _____, manipulating, pouting, pleading, demanding, nagging, etc.

2. Proverbs describes her as "quarrelsome" and "contentious"; both of these words come from the Hebrew root word *adon* which means sovereign, i.e. _____ (human or divine), lord, master, root of _____ name, "Adoni."[8] *Prov. 19:13, 21:9, 21:19, 25:24*

3. Because of the fall, all women struggle with the desire to be Irritating Women; it's our _____ condition when we are controlled by the flesh. *Gen. 3:16*

How's that Irritating Woman working for you?

1. _____ Story *Num. 12:1–15*

2. _____ Story *2 Sam. 6:12–23*

3. _____ Story *Gen. 16:1–5*

What will work for you?

1. The Daughters of Zelophehad: *Num. 27:1–10*

    a. They took their _____ to those in _____.

    b. They stated their case _____, _____, and respectfully.

    c. They offered a _____ and a _____ _____.

    d. They _____ the _____ to the authorities.
        RESULTS: They received what they needed *and* _____ _____, too.

2. _____ Example *Joshua 15:13–19*

3. _____ Example *Philemon*

Week Five • THE CAPTIVATING WOMAN

Can a biblically beautiful woman be sensual, sexual, and (dare I say) seductive? Yes! And that's exactly what the **Captivating Woman**, our very first "Beauty Do" from the Proverbs, will be teaching us this week as we learn about the sensuous side of biblical beauty.

OK, I'm pretty sure I just heard a few of you wives say, "Great. An entire lesson on sex. The last thing I need is more pressure about sex." So, let me just say, I understand. Between juggling family, job, home, and church responsibilities, sex can become just one more chore on an already too long list. If that describes you, then all I'm asking is that you incline your heart to God right now and say, "Lord, you know all about my crazy, busy life. But whatever you have to say to me this week, I'm listening." An open heart like that is an invitation for God to do the miraculous. And a change in your attitude about sex would probably be pretty miraculous, am I right?

For all of you singles, this week's lesson will prepare you for the plans God may have in store for your future. Only a few months ago, I met a precious, fifty-year-old, never-been-married woman. Content in her singleness, she had a great job, a fantastic church family and friends, and absolutely no plans whatsoever to get married…until God brought a godly widower into her world. Now she's planning a wedding, and someday you may be, too.

If you're married, this week's study could be your husband's favorite lesson. By the end of this week, you may become one red hot, biblically beautiful Captivating Woman. For you singles, think of this week's lesson as Honeymoon 101, a one-week course to prepare you for a red hot, biblically beautiful honeymoon. But as every experienced Captivating Woman knows, the honeymoon is great, but sex is like wine: it improves with age. Growing old does have its benefits. Glory!

DAY ONE

1. Want to be prized, honored, and valued? Then seek wisdom. Those who prize her will also be rewarded by her. Begin this week's lesson by praying and asking God to give you wisdom in every area of your life, including the most intimate area, your sex life.

> *If you prize wisdom, she will exalt you.*
> *Embrace her and she will honor you.*
> *She will place a lovely wreath on your head;*
> *she will present you with a beautiful crown.*
> —Proverbs 4:8–9

King Solomon authored three books of the Bible: Proverbs, Ecclesiastes, and Song of Solomon. This week, we will spend some time in each of them.

But never forget that God is the ultimate author and inspiration of every word in the Bible, and I want you to keep that in mind all week long as you read and study. And who knows? By the end of this week, your concept of God and sex may be radically changed for the better.

2. The beautiful description of the Captivating Woman is found in Proverbs 5:18–19. Please read this passage, and answer the following questions:

> ¹⁸ *Let your wife be a fountain of blessing for you.*
> *Rejoice in the wife of your youth.*
> ¹⁹ *She is a loving doe, a graceful deer.*
> *Let her breasts satisfy you always.*
> *May you always be captivated by her love.*
> —Proverbs 5:18–19

a. In this passage, who is the Captivating Woman? How is she defined? Please circle your answer.

> a single woman   *or*   a wife

b. What does this passage and your previous answer reveal about the biblical boundaries for sex, and how does this conflict with our culture?

c.   How is the Captivating Woman described? Circle all of the descriptive words and phrases used to describe her in this passage.

Proverbs 5:18–19 is a pretty steamy passage. The words are infused with fire and intensity. But in reality, this passage is even more sensual in its original Hebrew language.

For example, the Hebrew word "loving" in verse 19 means the wife is a very desirable and passionate lover.[9] The word "love" at the conclusion of this verse is used repeatedly in Song of Solomon (which we'll study tomorrow), and it refers to "powerful, intimate love between a man and a woman."[10] This is the kind of love God calls us to give to our husbands, and it's much more than mere affection. It is fiery, hot *passion*.

You are about to read a couple of Old Testament passages that contain the same Hebrew words for "love" and "loving" as in Proverbs 5:19. Although these passages may be very familiar to you, what you've just studied may enable you to see them in a truer and deeper way.

3.   Using the definitions you just learned for "love" and "loving," read the following passages, and record what you learn about the relationships they describe:

a.   Genesis 24:67

b.   Genesis 29:20

Solomon uses several beautiful words and phrases to describe the Captivating Woman in Proverbs 5. You have discovered what two of them mean. But in order to really understand and emulate this woman, we need to study two more.

In verse 19, Solomon describes the Captivating Woman as "a graceful doe." You've probably witnessed the elegance, beauty, and gracefulness of a doe firsthand, and Solomon had all of these qualities in mind when he used this metaphor. But the word "graceful" also denotes "a sense of acceptance or preference,"[11] which gives us an even deeper understanding of this passage. It reveals the Captivating Woman graciously accepts her husband and gives him preference—preeminence—above every other earthly relationship.

This same Hebrew word is used to describe God's grace to us—grace we did not earn, grace we did not deserve, grace that loved and reached out to us in spite of our sin. Therefore, in one single phrase from Proverbs 5:19, Solomon is saying the Captivating Woman elegantly, beautifully, and graciously accepts her husband just as God accepts us, and she favors him with her love over every earthly rival.

Practically, this means that God wants us to accept our husbands as they are, and to stop focusing on their faults and trying to change them. It also means that He wants us to put our husbands before our children, our family, our friends, our jobs, and every responsibility and possession we have. The only relationship that supersedes our relationship with our husbands is our relationship with Christ (Matthew 10:37).

There's one more word we need to examine in this verse. Solomon says the wife in Proverbs 5:19 captivates her husband. But what does "captivate" mean? Very simply, it means to intoxicate with love.[12] This wife has an absolutely intoxicating effect upon her husband. The power and passion of her love literally makes him reel. The King James Bible translates this word as "ravished," and the New American Standard translates it as "exhilarated." But my favorite translation is the Amplified Bible which says the husband is "transported with delight in her love." Wow! Now that's some kind of woman and some kind of lovin'!

I have one more scripture that I'd like for you to examine today. Written by Solomon, this verse will give us greater perspective about love and marriage.

4. Read Ecclesiastes 9:9 (it's the very next book after Proverbs), and explain the instructions it gives and how long this love will endure.

5. How does the Captivating Woman view sex? Think about what you've learned about her today, and complete the following sentence by circling the correct answers:

The Captivating Woman views sex as:

another chore on the list	a passionate delight
a means of pleasure	a means of procreation
routine	exciting
joyous	shameful
highly satisfying	mostly frustrating
a tool to get what she wants	a gift to demonstrate her love
a priority	an occasional duty

6. Don't even think about skipping this question, dear sister. Put down your pen, bow your head, and ask God to speak to your heart about all that you've studied today. Quiet your heart. Listen for His still, small voice. Record your response to God.

reflect

_____

_____

_____

_____

• • • • •

DAY TWO

1. Take a few minutes to love yourself. Pray and ask God to enable you to acquire wisdom as you study His Word today.

pray

> *To acquire wisdom is to love oneself;*
> *people who cherish understanding will prosper.*
> —Proverbs 19:8

Yesterday, you read Solomon's amazing (and sizzling) description of the Captivating Woman in Proverbs 5. Today, you'll meet another woman who is a perfect example of a Captivating Woman. Solomon will introduce us to her as well.

If you have ever studied Solomon, you know that he was quite a ladies man. But in his greatest and favorite work, the Song of Solomon, he extols only one woman. Although her name never appears in his Song, Solomon affectionately and repeatedly refers to her as his "beloved," and his "darling."

Song of Solomon is autobiographical. Throughout the book, Solomon refers to himself as the "king," the "lover," and the "bridegroom." But this book is far more than an autobiography. Song of Solomon is an inspired poem that magnifies, celebrates, and applauds the beauty of love, courtship, and marriage. May the inspiration on its pages inspire and encourage you as you read, study, and observe it today and tomorrow.

2. Slowly and purposefully, read and study following passages from Song of Solomon (also called the Song of Songs in some translations of the Bible).

   Using the following abbreviations, make notes in the margins beside verses that describe ways in which the young man and woman use the five senses to express their love and to fuel the fire of love:

   SI = Sight   Use this abbreviation when you notice how they visually stimulate and physically attract one another.

   T = Touch: Use this abbreviation when you notice how they use touch to demonstrate and express their love.

   H = Hearing: Use this abbreviation when you notice how they use words to express their love for one another.

   S = Smell   Use this abbreviation when you notice how they use fragrance and smell to attract and enhance love.

   TA = Taste   Use this abbreviation when you notice how they use taste to enhance love.

Song of Songs 1–2 *(NLT)*

¹ This is Solomon's song of songs, more wonderful than any other.

Young Woman

> *² Kiss me and kiss me again, for your love is sweeter than wine.*
>
> *³ How fragrant your cologne; your name is like its spreading fragrance. No wonder all the young women love you!*
>
> *⁴ Take me with you; come, let's run! The king has brought me into his bedroom.*

Young Women of Jerusalem

> *How happy we are for you, O king. We praise your love even more than wine.*

Young Woman

> *How right they are to adore you.*
>
> *⁵ I am dark but beautiful, O women of Jerusalem—dark as the tents of Kedar, dark as the curtains of Solomon's tents.*
>
> *⁶ Don't stare at me because I am dark—the sun has darkened my skin. My brothers were angry with me; they forced me to care for their vineyards, so I couldn't care for myself—my own vineyard.*
>
> *⁷ Tell me, my love, where are you leading your flock today? Where will you rest your sheep at noon? For why should I wander like a prostitute among your friends and their flocks?*

Young Man

> *⁸ If you don't know, O most beautiful woman, follow the trail of my flock, and graze your young goats by the shepherds' tents.*
>
> *⁹ You are as exciting, my darling, as a mare among Pharaoh's stallions.*
>
> *¹⁰ How lovely are your cheeks; your earrings set them afire! How lovely is your neck, enhanced by a string of jewels.*
>
> *¹¹ We will make for you earrings of gold and beads of silver.*

Young Woman

> *¹² The king is lying on his couch, enchanted by the fragrance of my perfume.*
>
> *¹³ My lover is like a sachet of myrrh lying between my breasts.*
>
> *¹⁴ He is like a bouquet of sweet henna blossoms from the vineyards of En-gedi.*

Young Man

> *¹⁵ How beautiful you are, my darling, how beautiful! Your eyes are like doves.*

Young Woman

> *¹⁶ You are so handsome, my love, pleasing beyond words! The soft grass is our bed;*
>
> *¹⁷ fragrant cedar branches are the beams of our house, and pleasant smelling firs are the rafters.*
>
> *²:¹ I am the spring crocus blooming on the Sharon Plain, the lily of the valley.*

Young Man

> ² *Like a lily among thistles is my darling among young women.*

Young Woman

> ³ *Like the finest apple tree in the orchard is my lover among other young men.*
>   *I sit in his delightful shade and taste his delicious fruit.*
> ⁴ *He escorts me to the banquet hall; it's obvious how much he loves me.*
> ⁵ *Strengthen me with raisin cakes, refresh me with apples, for I am weak with love.*
> ⁶ *His left arm is under my head, and his right arm embraces me.*
> ⁷ *Promise me, O women of Jerusalem, by the gazelles and wild deer, not to awaken*
>   *love until the time is right.*
> ⁸ *Ah, I hear my lover coming! He is leaping over the mountains, bounding over*
>   *the hills.*
> ⁹ *My lover is like a swift gazelle or a young stag. Look, there he is behind the wall,*
>   *looking through the window, peering into the room.*
> ¹⁰ *My lover said to me, "Rise up, my darling! Come away with me, my fair one!*
> ¹¹ *Look, the winter is past, and the rains are over and gone.*
> ¹² *The flowers are springing up, the season of singing birds has come, and the cooing*
>   *of turtledoves fills the air.*
> ¹³ *The fig trees are forming young fruit, and the fragrant grapevines are blossoming.*
>   *Rise up, my darling! Come away with me, my fair one!"*

Young Man

> ¹⁴ *My dove is hiding behind the rocks, behind an outcrop on the cliff. Let me see*
>   *your face; let me hear your voice. For your voice is pleasant, and your face is lovely.*

Young Women of Jerusalem

> ¹⁵ *Catch all the foxes, those little foxes, before they ruin the vineyard of love, for the*
>   *grapevines are blossoming!*

Young Woman

> ¹⁶ *My lover is mine, and I am his. He browses among the lilies.*
> ¹⁷ *Before the dawn breezes blow and the night shadows flee, return to me, my love,*
>   *like a gazelle or a young stag on the rugged mountains.*

3. Is there a message for singles in Song of Solomon 2:7? What do you think this verse means?

4. Song of Solomon 2:15 refers to the "little foxes" that "ruin the vineyard of love". What are some of the things that ruin and prevent love from blossoming in courtship and in marriage? What can quench the flame of love between a man and a woman?

5. What has the Captivating Woman in Solomon's Song taught you today?

reflect

_____

_____

_____

_____

• • • • •

DAY THREE

1. According to today's Proverb, getting wisdom is a priority. As you continue your study on the Captivating Woman, pray and ask God to give you wisdom in your most intimate earthly relationships. Commit to take what He's already taught you and apply it to your life today.

Getting wisdom is the most important thing you can do!
—Proverbs 4:7

As you have learned in previous weeks, a biblically beautiful woman is pure, discreet, prudent, and edifying—but that's not all. A biblically beautiful woman is also passionate, erotic, and romantic. Within the bounds of marriage, God encourages us to unlock sexual desire and to unleash its power in a way that captivates our husbands.

Today you will study two more chapters from Song of Solomon. It's easy to see why Solomon favored it above all of the other books and songs he wrote. I hope it's becoming one of your favorites, too. Enjoy!

2. Just like yesterday, slowly and purposefully read the following passages from Song of Solomon. Make notes in the margins using the same abbreviations you used yesterday.

SI = Sight   Use this abbreviation when you notice how they visually stimulate and physically attract one another.

T = Touch: Use this abbreviation when you notice how they use touch to demonstrate and express their love.

H = Hearing: Use this abbreviation when you notice how they use words to express their love for one another.

S = Smell   Use this abbreviation when you notice how they use fragrance and smell to attract and enhance love.

TA = Taste   Use this abbreviation when you notice how they use taste to enhance love.

Song of Songs 4:1–5:1 *(NLT)*

Young Man
> *¹ You are beautiful, my darling, beautiful beyond words. Your eyes are like doves behind your veil. Your hair falls in waves, like a flock of goats winding down the slopes of Gilead.*
> *² Your teeth are as white as sheep, recently shorn and freshly washed. Your smile is flawless, each tooth matched with its twin.*
> *³ Your lips are like scarlet ribbon; your mouth is inviting. Your cheeks are like rosy pomegranates behind your veil.*
> *⁴ Your neck is as beautiful as the tower of David, jeweled with the shields of a thousand heroes.*
> *⁵ Your breasts are like two fawns, twin fawns of a gazelle grazing among the lilies.*
> *⁶ Before the dawn breezes blow and the night shadows flee, I will hurry to the mountain of myrrh and to the hill of frankincense.*
> *⁷ You are altogether beautiful, my darling, beautiful in every way.*

⁸ *Come with me from Lebanon, my bride, come with me from Lebanon. Come down from Mount Amana, from the peaks of Senir and Hermon, where the lions have their dens and leopards live among the hills.*

⁹ *You have captured my heart, my treasure, my bride. You hold it hostage with one glance of your eyes, with a single jewel of your necklace.*

¹⁰ *Your love delights me, my treasure, my bride. Your love is better than wine, your perfume more fragrant than spices.*

¹¹ *Your lips are as sweet as nectar, my bride. Honey and milk are under your tongue. Your clothes are scented like the cedars of Lebanon.*

¹² *You are my private garden, my treasure, my bride, a secluded spring, a hidden fountain.*

¹³ *Your thighs shelter a paradise of pomegranates with rare spices—henna with nard,*

¹⁴ *nard and saffron, fragrant calamus and cinnamon, with all the trees of frankincense, myrrh, and aloes, and every other lovely spice.*

¹⁵ *You are a garden fountain, a well of fresh water streaming down from Lebanon's mountains.*

Young Woman

¹⁶ *Awake, north wind! Rise up, south wind! Blow on my garden and spread its fragrance all around. Come into your garden, my love; taste its finest fruits.*

Young Man

^{5:1} *I have entered my garden, my treasure, my bride! I gather myrrh with my spices and eat honeycomb with my honey. I drink wine with my milk.*

Young Women of Jerusalem

Oh, lover and beloved, eat and drink! Yes, drink deeply of your love!

<u>Song of Songs 7:1–13</u> *(NLT)*

Young Man

¹ *How beautiful are your sandaled feet, O queenly maiden. Your rounded thighs are like jewels, the work of a skilled craftsman.*

² *Your navel is perfectly formed like a goblet filled with mixed wine. Between your thighs lies a mound of wheat bordered with lilies.*

³ *Your breasts are like two fawns, twin fawns of a gazelle.*

⁴ *Your neck is as beautiful as an ivory tower. Your eyes are like the sparkling pools in Heshbon by the gate of Bath-rabbim. Your nose is as fine as the tower of Lebanon overlooking Damascus.*

⁵ *Your head is as majestic as Mount Carmel, and the sheen of your hair radiates royalty. The king is held captive by its tresses.*

⁶ *Oh, how beautiful you are! How pleasing, my love, how full of delights!*

⁷ *You are slender like a palm tree, and your breasts are like its clusters of fruit.*

> [8] *I said, "I will climb the palm tree and take hold of its fruit." May your breasts*
> *be like grape clusters, and the fragrance of your breath like apples.*
> [9] *May your kisses be as exciting as the best wine, flowing gently over lips and teeth.*

Young Woman

> [10] *I am my lover's, and he claims me as his own.*
> [11] *Come, my love, let us go out to the fields and spend the night among the*
> *wildflowers.*
> [12] *Let us get up early and go to the vineyards to see if the grapevines have budded,*
> *if the blossoms have opened, and if the pomegranates have bloomed. There I will*
> *give you my love.*
> [13] *There the mandrakes give off their fragrance, and the finest fruits are at our door,*
> *new delights as well as old, which I have saved for you, my lover.*

I hope God is using the Song of Solomon to rev up your attitude about sex if you're married, and to prepare you for a possible honeymoon if you're single. Some of you wives may even be inspired to add some new lingerie to your wardrobe (my husband keeps me on a pretty tight budget, but there's *always* money for sexy lingerie) or to pick up some sensual-smelling body potions.

The Captivating Young Woman in Song of Solomon appealed to all of Solomon's senses. She looks good, smells good, sounds good, feels good—she even tastes good. This chick may have been young, but she was one wise girl. We can learn a lot from her, and I think that's one of the primary reasons God inspired this book: He wants us to put it into practice in our own bedrooms.

One of the best books I've read lately is *Intimate Issues: 21 Questions Christian Women Ask About Sex* by Linda Dillow and Lorraine Pintus. They believe the Captivating Young Woman in Song of Solomon is a role model for Christian wives, and they note five specific qualities we can learn from her: (1) she is responsive (Song 4:16); (2) she is adventurous (Song 7:11-13); (3) she is uninhibited (Song 2:6, 4:16, 7:1–3); (4) she is expressive (Song 1:16, 2:3, 16); and (5) she is sensuous (Song 5:10–16).[13] So, dear sister, how can you build these five qualities and the five senses into your love life? Good question, huh? Get ready to answer it.

3. Using Song of Solomon as your guide and your imagination and creativity as well, record one or two (or three or four if you like) responses in each of the spaces on the following charts. To help you get started, I've provided some "starters" on each chart. Even if you're not married, answer these questions as though you were.

5 Qualities of a Modern-Day Captivating Woman

She demonstrates responsiveness to her husband by:

Smiling and responding positively to his touch instead of protesting.

She demonstrates adventurousness to her husband by:

Secretly enlisting a babysitter and planning an all-night getaway.

She demonstrates her lack of inhibitions to her husband by:

Enjoying undressing herself as he watches.

She demonstrates her expressiveness to her husband by:

Telling him how he sexually pleases her as they make love.

She demonstrates her sensuousness to her husband by:

Seducing him with just a look.

Creative Ways the Captivating Woman Uses the 5 Senses

Sight

She takes care of her appearance especially at bedtime.

Touch

She strokes his arm (and maybe his thigh) while he's driving.

Hear

She plays CDs and love songs they both enjoy.

Smell

She knows what his favorite fragrance is, and she wears it to bed each night.

Taste

She enjoys feeding him bites of sweet fruit or chocolate.

4. What are the top three things the Lord has shown you through the Song of Solomon?

reflect

_____

_____

_____

_____

· · · · ·

DAY FOUR

1. Begin your time of study today by praying and thanking God for the way His wisdom has protected and guarded you in the past. Ask Him to use the wisdom He is giving you this week to guard and to protect your future.

pray

> *Don't turn your back on wisdom, for she will protect you.*
> *Love her, and she will guard you.*
> —Proverbs 4:6

Jesus affirmed the importance of sexuality and oneness in marriage when He said, "Have you not read that He who created them from the beginning MADE THEM MALE AND FEMALE, and said, 'FOR THIS REASON A MAN SHALL LEAVE HIS FATHER AND MOTHER AND BE JOINED TO HIS WIFE, AND THE TWO SHALL BECOME ONE FLESH'? So they are no longer two, but one flesh. What therefore God has joined together, let no man separate" (Matthew 19:3–6).

Christ not only upheld the sexual relationship of marriage, He hallowed and made it sacred. While the world debases, dishonors, and degrades sex, God's Word glorifies and upholds it as an act of holiness to be enjoyed and shared by a husband and wife.

Today we will learn more about becoming biblically beautiful Captivating Women as we move into the New Testament and study several key passages on the sacredness of marriage and sexuality.

2. Read Ephesians 5:22–32, and answer the following questions:

    a. How are wives to submit themselves to their husbands (verses 22, 24).

    b. How are husbands to lead their wives (verses 23, 25, 28)?

    c. What relationship does marriage symbolize?

    d. What does sex symbolize (verses 30–32)?

Over the past few days, we have seen one of God's primary purposes for creating sex: pleasure. God wants us to enjoy sex—to the point that it "intoxicates" us. God also created sex for procreation (Genesis 1:28), partnership (Genesis 2:18), protection (1 Corinthians 7:9), and to provide comfort (Genesis 24:67, 2 Samuel 12:24).

But what I want you to see today is that God also created sex to be an earthly picture of Christ's relationship with us, His church. This means God sees sexual intimacy as something serious, sacred, and significant.

Solomon's writings have encouraged us to enjoy the passionate pleasures of sex. But the New Testament passages we are about to study will remind us of the sacredness of sex.

3. Read the following passages, and record what they teach about sex, its biblical boundaries, and how to keep it sacred:

    a. Matthew 5:27–28

    b. 1 Corinthians 6:9

    c. 1 Corinthians 6:13, 18–20

    d. 1 Thessalonians 4:3–7

    e. Hebrews 13:4

While the passages you just read give an overview of the biblical boundaries of sex and address such things as immorality, adultery, lust, and homosexuality, you still may have questions about specific sexual practices between husbands and wives. In *Intimate Issues*, the book I referred to yesterday, the authors encourage married couples to seek God's wisdom and to ask the following three questions as they consider a specific sexual practice:

1) Is it prohibited in Scripture? If not, we may assume it is permitted. "Everything is permissible for me" (1 Cor. 6:12 *NIV*).

2) Is it beneficial? Does the practice in any way harm the husband or wife or hinder the sexual relationship? If so, it should be rejected. "Everything is permissible for me—but not everything is beneficial" (1 Cor. 6:12 *NIV*).

3) Does it involve anyone else? Sexual activity is sanctioned by God for husband and wife only. If a sexual practice involves someone else or becomes public, it is wrong based on Hebrews 13:4, which warns us to keep the marriage bed undefiled.[14]

There is, however, one other prohibition regarding sex, and it is a widespread problem in many marriages. Our final New Testament passage for today will address this issue very thoroughly.

4. Read 1 Corinthians 7:3–5, and answer the following questions:

a. What are husbands and wives commanded to do (verse 3)?

b. What are husbands and wives commanded not to do (verse 5)?

c. What exception is given to this command (verse 5)?

d. What are the possible repercussions of disobeying this command (verse 5)?

e. What reasons do wives often use to excuse themselves from sex?

f. Can you think of some valid reasons why a husband or wife would be unable to have sex? If so, what would they be?

5. How has God used His Word to speak to you today?

reflect

_____

_____

_____

_____

• • • • •

DAY FIVE

pray

1. If we trust the world's beliefs about sex (or even what seems perfectly sensible to us) we will place ourselves and our futures in danger. Spend a few minutes in prayer, and commit to walk in the truths of the wisdom God has revealed to you this week.

Trusting oneself is foolish, but those who walk in wisdom are safe.
—Proverbs 28:26

Years ago, I was teaching a women's Bible study class, and our topic was sex. We discussed many of the same things you have studied this week. After the class was dismissed, a young woman came up and confessed to me that she did not enjoy sex; and (as you can imagine) it was a huge point of contention between she and her husband, who was not a Christian. I prayed with her, encouraged her, and let her borrow a wonderful (and explicit) Christian book about sex that I had brought to class with me that day.

The very next week, she returned to class a changed woman. She joyously reported that after she read the truths and principles in the book I gave to her, she was able to approach sex and her husband in a completely different way. She also told me that her husband enjoyed reading the book, too. But she had even better news: after enjoying just a few short days of sexual bliss with his wife, that unbelieving husband told her he would like to start attending church with her. Girl, that's the power of a Captivating Woman and a miracle-working God!

At the conclusion of this week's lesson, I'll give you the name of the Christian sex manual I let that young woman borrow (she did give it back—she told me she'd purchased her own copy!). But if you are married to an unbelieving husband, let me encourage you to do what that young woman did. Win him to the Lord without a word. Win him to the Lord through your behavior— especially your loving, accepting sexual behavior toward him (1 Peter 3:1).

In today's homework, I will point you to a passage that has tremendous application for all of us as we pursue biblical beauty. But first, I want to focus on some very positive principles for those of you who are single.

2. Paul, who was a committed Christian single, specifically addresses singles in 1 Corinthians 7:7–9, 32–35. Read these verses, and answer the following questions:

   a. According to Paul, what gift had God given him that he wished others had?

   b. What counsel did Paul give to singles (verses 8–9)?
      NOTE: The word burn in verse 9 means to burn with lust.

    c. You have seen the positive aspects about marriage and sex this week, but what are the positive aspects of remaining single (verses 32–35)?

    d. According to these verses, what relationship should a Christian single focus on?

    Two precious single women who piloted this study with me recommended two great Christian books that ministered to them. The first book is *Passion and Purity* by Elisabeth Elliot. As she shares from her own personal letters, diaries, and memories, Elisabeth shares the temptations and the victories she experienced as a Christian single who longed to please the Lord.

    The second book is *Surrender: The Heart God Controls* by Nancy Leigh DeMoss (a committed Christian single herself). If you're struggling with being single (or difficult circumstances, a lack of joy, etc.), this book will teach you how to discover victory by living a life that is fully surrendered to God. Although I haven't read either of these books, I've read other books by these authors and they were fantastic. And based upon the rave reviews of my two single friends, *Passion and Purity* and *Surrender* sound like must-reads—I plan to pick them up soon and enjoy a good read myself! Hope you'll do the same.

3. Your final passage of study this week is a familiar one: 1 Corinthians 13:4–8. Read this passage and, as you read, think about how it applies to your marriage or to other close relationships you have. Next, personalize and pray this passage to the Lord asking him to build these characteristics of love into your life, your marriage, and your relationships.

4. Has the Lord, perhaps, changed your heart and attitude in any way this week? Has His Word encouraged you to take specific action as a single or married woman? Conclude your week of study by taking time to answer these questions by journaling.

My Journal

This week the Lord...

_____

_____

_____

_____

_____

I grew up in the 1960s and 70s during the heyday of the so-called "sexual revolution." Immorality was "in," and marriage was "out." Everybody seemed to be talking about sex except the church. Even the word "sex" was considered dirty by many Christians. It was the dark ages. Books on biblical sexuality were rare, and they were purposefully placed on shelves where no one could see or reach them.

But in 1976, another revolution began when a Christian pastor and his wife authored an explicit book on biblical sexuality. That book was *The Act of Marriage: The Beauty of Sexual Love*, by Tim and Beverly LaHaye. It flew off the shelves of Christian book stores and ushered in an era of enlightened, biblical knowledge about sex that many Christians had never known before. Including me.

Back then, good Christian women didn't discuss sex, much less write about the art and pleasures of making love. But thank God, Beverly LaHaye stepped up and changed all of that; and I for one am greatly indebted to her. But I'm not the only one. Remember that woman in my Bible study class? Yes, it was my dog-eared copy of *The Act of Marriage* that changed her life and marriage.

With more than 2.5 million copies in print, *The Act of Marriage* has become a Christian classic. Furthermore, it has paved the way for many other great books and resources about sex to be widely available today for Christians—and sometimes for their unbelieving spouses. We have Tim LaHaye and his biblically beautiful, captivating wife, Beverly, to thank for that.

Week Five • THE ABC'S OF THE CAPTIVATING WOMAN

Introduction: What Sex Means to a Man and What Sex Means to a Woman from *The Act of Marriage* by Tim and Beverly LaHaye.

<u>Man</u>   <u>Woman</u>

- _____
- _____
- _____
- _____
- _____

- _____
- _____
- _____
- _____
- _____

1. *A*_____ Song of Solomon 1

2. *B*_____ Song of Solomon 1:10–12, 4:11

3. *C*_____ Song of Solomon 2:8–9, 5:9–16, 7

4. *C*_____ Song of Solomon 1:7–17, 2:10–13

5. *C*_____ Song of Solomon 4:10–16

Week Six • THE IDEAL WOMAN

Dessert has always been my favorite course—even if it's just a couple of Oreos® after a peanut butter and banana sandwich. Some say, "Life's short. Eat dessert first." But not me. I like saving the best for last. And that is exactly how I feel about this final lesson on Beauty Do #2, the **Ideal Woman**. Of all of the women presented in Proverbs, she is the best, so Proverbs saves her as its final and most satisfying course.

But the Ideal Woman is no fancy cream puff or sugar-filled bonbon. She is a woman of substance. She leads a purposeful and significant life. And although she wears many hats and juggles many responsibilities, she balances the various aspects of her life with wisdom, prudence, and integrity.

While I was in the big middle of writing this Bible study, one of my favorite friends called to encourage me. She said, "I really like that you used the word 'becoming' in the subtitle of the study. I like that word. It reminds me that biblical beauty is a process." To be honest, I hadn't even considered that, but I was so grateful God revealed it to her and led her to share it with me.

Biblical beauty is, indeed, a process. So don't be intimidated by the Ideal Woman this week. Even she had to go through the process of "becoming." And if she made it, girl, we can, too. Here's to "becoming."

DAY ONE

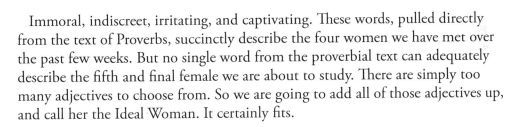

1. If you're a sweet-a-holic like I am, you're going to love today's Proverb! Pray today, asking God to make this week's lesson a sweet treat and a delicious dessert of wisdom from His Word.

> *My child, eat honey, for it is good,*
> *and the honeycomb is sweet to the taste.*
> *In the same way, wisdom is sweet to your soul.*
> *If you find it, you will have a bright future,*
> *and your hopes will not be cut short.*
> —Proverbs 24:13–14

Immoral, indiscreet, irritating, and captivating. These words, pulled directly from the text of Proverbs, succinctly describe the four women we have met over the past few weeks. But no single word from the proverbial text can adequately describe the fifth and final female we are about to study. There are simply too many adjectives to choose from. So we are going to add all of those adjectives up, and call her the Ideal Woman. It certainly fits.

As we browse and study through Proverbs 31 this week, let's be sure to "try on" some of these adjectives ourselves. And trust me—they'll fit. That's one of my favorite things about God's Word. Every verse is one-size-fits-all. Makes "becoming" an Ideal Woman seem even more doable!

2. Read all about the Ideal Woman in the following passage:

Proverbs 31:10–31 *(NLT)*

> ¹⁰ *Who can find a virtuous and capable wife? She is more precious than rubies.*
> ¹¹ *Her husband can trust her, and she will greatly enrich his life.*
> ¹² *She brings him good, not harm, all the days of her life.*
> ¹³ *She finds wool and flax and busily spins it.*
> ¹⁴ *She is like a merchant's ship, bringing her food from afar.*
> ¹⁵ *She gets up before dawn to prepare breakfast for her household and plan the day's work for her servant girls.*
> ¹⁶ *She goes to inspect a field and buys it; with her earnings she plants a vineyard.*
> ¹⁷ *She is energetic and strong, a hard worker.*
> ¹⁸ *She makes sure her dealings are profitable; her lamp burns late into the night.*
> ¹⁹ *Her hands are busy spinning thread, her fingers twisting fiber.*
> ²⁰ *She extends a helping hand to the poor and opens her arms to the needy.*

[21] She has no fear of winter for her household, for everyone has warm clothes.

[22] She makes her own bedspreads. She dresses in fine linen and purple gowns.

[23] Her husband is well known at the city gates, where he sits with the other civic leaders.

[24] She makes belted linen garments and sashes to sell to the merchants.

[25] She is clothed with strength and dignity, and she laughs without fear of the future.

[26] When she speaks, her words are wise, and she gives instructions with kindness.

[27] She carefully watches everything in her household and suffers nothing from laziness.

[28] Her children stand and bless her. Her husband praises her:

[29] "There are many virtuous and capable women in the world, but you surpass them all!"

[30] Charm is deceptive, and beauty does not last; but a woman who fears the Lord will be greatly praised.

[31] Reward her for all she has done. Let her deeds publicly declare her praise.

3. Using words from the text of Proverbs 31, record some of the primary characteristics of the Ideal Woman.

The very first word used to describe the Ideal Woman is "virtuous". To some, this word may conjure up a picture of someone who is way too perfect, who wears a giant halo, and has no fun whatsoever. But that's not what "virtuous" means at all. What it actually means is strength, influence, and character.[15] The Ideal Woman is a strong woman, an influential woman, and a woman whose character empowers her in every area of her life. As a result, she is successful and respected. But who are her biggest fans? Let's take a look and see.

4. How does the Ideal Woman's husband feel about her, and why does he feel this way?

5. What role do you think the Ideal Woman may have had in her husband's success (verse 23)? How does a woman like this benefit her husband in his profession?

6. Proverbs has a lot to say about wives. Take a look at the following verses, and record what you learn about how a wife can bless (or harm) her husband:

    a. Proverbs 12:4

    b. Proverbs 18:22

    c. Proverbs 19:14

7. According to Proverbs 31:28, how do the Ideal Woman's children feel about her, and why would they feel this way?

8. All moms want to have children who respect and honor them. Proverbs has so much wisdom to help us achieve these goals. Read the following verses, and record what they teach:

    a. Proverbs 13:24, 29:15, 17

    b. Proverbs 22:6

    c. Proverbs 31:1–9

9. Select one of the following questions, and record your response:

    •   Whose praise do you most desire, and what have you learned today to enable you to receive it?

    •   Describe an Ideal Woman you've known and how she has influenced you.

    _____

    _____

    _____

    _____

DAY TWO

1. Wisdom enables us to build our homes and to build up the people we love. Sadly, we have all witnessed the opposite and destructive effect of those who choose to ignore wisdom. Ask God to give you wisdom to build your home, your family, and those you love today.

> *A wise woman builds her home,*
> *but a foolish woman tears it down with her own hands.*
> —Proverbs 14:1

    Biblical beauty is reflected through our homes and the way we care for them. Today, we will continue our study of Proverbs 31 and focus on the home management skills of the Ideal Woman.

    If you need a little inspiration (as I do) to help you become a more biblically beautiful homekeeper, I think you'll find the Ideal Woman tops Martha Stewart hands down. And I especially like the fact that our gal from the Proverbs never once utters the word "perfect"—and that really is "a good thing."

2. Using the Proverbs 31 passage in yesterday's lesson, compile a list of the responsibilities the Ideal Woman oversees and performs for her home and household.
   NOTE: Don't include her business/job responsibilities. We'll study that aspect of her work tomorrow.

Homekeeping Responsibilities	

3. Yesterday you learned the word "virtuous" means strength and character.[16] What kind of strengths would a woman need to accomplish the tasks on the list you just compiled in Question 2? In other words, what necessary skills and character traits are required to manage a successful home and family?

4. Read Proverbs 31:21, 25, and answer the following questions:

    a. Why does the Ideal Woman have such a positive outlook about the future? How can she be so confident?

    b. What practical things can you do to prepare your home and family for the future and for the possibility of hard times?

5. How does the condition of your house affect you and your family? What difference does a clean and orderly or messy and disorganized house make? Think about these questions, and list five benefits of a clean house and five hindrances of a messy house. I've given you a couple of my own answers to help you get started.

The Upside of a Clean House	The Downside of a Messy House
I can find things when I need them.	*I feel overwhelmed and stressed.*
1.	1.
2.	2.
3.	3.
4.	4.
5.	5.

I am sure you noticed the Ideal Woman had "servant girls" (plural even) to help her. You may not have even one "servant girl," but you probably have a washer and dryer, a dishwasher, and many other modern conveniences (don't forget about running water and electricity) that the Ideal Woman in Proverbs 31 did not have.

Also, if you have children, they need to be trained to help and serve around the house. I used to fuss, mope, and seethe at my mother for making me do chores around the house. But I am so glad she was unfazed by my pouting. Mother held her ground, made me work, and never let me get by with a second-rate effort. I couldn't "clock out" until I passed her inspection. Because of her strength and fortitude, she managed to teach me how to keep a proper house despite the fact that I was an unwilling student.

But do not—do not—get the idea that my mother's house or mine is perfect. If you ask me, a house that must be kept perfectly clean and perfectly organized at all times is over-the-top, and Sandra Felton (author of *The Messies Manual: A Complete Guide to Bringing Order and Beauty to Your Home*) agrees with me. Sandra, a self-proclaimed former Messie, says we shouldn't aim to keep a perfect house like a "Cleanie" (as she calls perfectionistic housekeepers). Instead, she encourages women to become "Successful Average Housekeepers," which she defines as follows:

> [Successful Average Housekeepers do] not take housekeeping nearly as seriously as the Cleanies and [do] not work at it with as much discipline as they do. Nonetheless, their homes are always neat enough. They are not suffering from clutter overload because they know a few basic organizational principles and consistently apply them. The result: a consistently okay house.[17]

Sandra uses a 0–10 scale to rate levels of housekeeping. A 0 ranking means "no one cares to enter your house."[18] A level 10 ranking means "no one dares to enter your house."[19] I don't want to be a 0 or a 10, do you? And I tend to think that's the way the Ideal Woman felt, too.

I imagine the Ideal Woman's home was mostly clean and well-ordered and her pantry was pretty full and well-stocked. If unexpected company dropped by, I think she was happy (not embarrassed) to see them, and she invited them to come in without hesitation. I don't think they had to remove their shoes at the door, stay off the good furniture, or remain inside the kitchen when she offered them a cup of coffee either.

Don't get me wrong, I do think housekeeping is important. It is certainly one aspect of biblical beauty. But there are far more important things we must give priority to in our homes, and one of them is "heartkeeping."

Finally, Guilt-free Help for Messies!

Need help conquering your clutter?

Ready to get your house clean and under control?

Find practical help and fabulous resources
by visiting

Sandra Felton's

Messies Anonymous website

at

www.messies.com/site/

6. Read the following verse, and record two or three practical things you can do to keep your heart and home "clean."

> *I will lead a life of integrity in my own home.*
> *I will refuse to look at anything vile and vulgar.*
> —Psalm 101:2–3

7. How are things at your house, and how has the Lord spoken to you about it today?

reflect

_____

_____

_____

. . . . .

DAY THREE

1. Wisdom + good sense = a strong house. Today, ask God to give you both wisdom and good sense.

pray

> *A house is built by wisdom and*
> *becomes strong through good sense.*
> —Proverbs 24:3

What does God's Word say about wives and moms working outside the home? It is a controversial question, and there is no shortage of opinions on this subject. So, today let's look at this topic as objectively as possible and allow God's Word to do all the talking. I will neither preach nor push my own personal interpretations about the passages we are about to study—and I will ask you to do the same. Together let us say, "Spirit speak."

2. Use the Proverbs 31 passage in your Day One homework (or in your Bible if you prefer to use it) to answer the following questions:

   a. Does the Ideal Woman work outside the home? Circle your answer.

      Yes   No

   b. With regard to your previous answer, list the specific scriptural evidence you based your answer upon. Be as thorough as possible in your answer.

   c. What did you learn about her schedule (verses 15, 18), and how would it have affected her family and other responsibilities?

   d. What did scriptural evidence did you find about her work ethic, and how would that have affected her family and other responsibilities?

   e. How did her income impact her family and others? What did you learn about the way she manage her finances?

f. Overall, what scriptural evidence did you see about the priorities of the Ideal Woman?

3. Proverbs has a lot to say about work, and we all have some kind of work to do. Read the scriptures on the following chart, and record what they teach about the consequences of laziness and the rewards of hard work.

The Consequences of Laziness vs. Rewards of Hard Work
Proverbs 12:24
Proverbs 13:4
Proverbs 15:19
Proverbs 21:5
Proverbs 28:19

I knew a wonderful Christian mom who posted scriptures from Proverbs (like the ones you just read) on a chalkboard in her kitchen. She updated the scriptures frequently. And sometimes she put great quotes from famous Christians on the chalkboard, too. Ideal Women find practical and creative ways to teach and train their children, and she was certainly one of them. Got some kids (or grandkids) at your house? Get yourself a chalkboard, girl!

4. How has the Lord spoken to you today, and how will you respond to what He has shown you?

_____

_____

_____

_____

• • • • •

DAY FOUR

1. Before you begin today's lesson, thank God for the wise women He has placed in your life. Ask Him to make you a beacon of His wisdom to other women.

> *Wisdom is enshrined in an understanding heart;*
> *wisdom is not found among fools.*
> —Proverbs 14:33

Today we will discover another facet of biblical beauty from the Ideal Woman. It is my heart's desire and prayer that this lesson will prepare you for the opportunities and open doors God has for your life and future.

2. As you have seen in previous lessons this week, the Ideal Woman ministers to her family and household in many ways. But others benefit from her life and ministry as well. Read Proverbs 31:20, 26, and answer the following questions:

a. How does the Ideal Woman bless and minister to others?

b. As you think about the Ideal Woman's example in verse 20, what are some practical, everyday ways you can minister to others as she did?

c. As you think about the Ideal Woman's example in verse 26, what opportunities has God given you to instruct and give wisdom to others?

One of the casualties of a crazy schedule and a busy lifestyle is that we become so preoccupied with our own lives and responsibilities that we become blind to the needs of others. Yet in the midst of a very busy lifestyle, the Ideal Woman remains sensitive to the needs of those around her. In Proverbs 31, we see two specific ways she ministers to those needs: 1) through her words, and 2) through her deeds.

Before we learn the specific way the Ideal Woman uses her words to minister to others, let find out what Proverbs has to say about the blessings of ministering through our deeds to the poor.

3. Read the following passages, and record what they teach about ministering to others through our generosity and deeds:

a. Proverbs 14:31

b. Proverbs 19:17

    c.   Proverbs 28:27

    d.   Proverbs 31:9

The second way the Ideal Woman ministers to others is through her speech. In Proverbs 31:26, her words are described as "wise," which means she speaks with "knowledge, experience, intelligence, insight, and judgment."[20] She's the kind of woman other women respect (men, too), and her wise counsel is sought and prized.

Proverbs 31:26 also says that "she gives instructions with kindness" *(NLT)*. The King James Version says it like this: "in her tongue is the law of kindness." But what is the "law of kindness"? And what instructions is she giving? Well, I discovered two beautiful Hebrew words when I studied this verse: the first is "torah" and the second is "hesed." Let me give you the scoop.

The word for "law" *(KJV)* and "instructions" *(NLT)* is the Hebrew word "torah," a very familiar word to every Jew. When they use this word, they are usually referring to the first five books of the Old Testament known as the Law. But "torah" also has a broader and more general meaning. In Proverbs 31:26, it means "instruction, doctrine and teaching."[21] Therefore, the instructions the Ideal Woman gives are spiritual and meaningful.

"Hesed" (the Hebrew word translated "kindness" in this passage) is rooted in one of the "most important words in the Old Testament, and is often translated in the KJV as 'lovingkindness' or 'mercy.'"[22] Hesed is a quality central to God's character,"[23] and "it is the foundation for God's actions."[24]

Dear sister, I know these definitions are a little tedious, but they expand and clarify God's calling on our lives in a specific way. In our conversations and daily encounters with others, God's goal is that our words will minister wisdom to others. But there's more: God is calling us to spiritually teach and instruct others, and the central message of our teaching must be love, His love. What a high calling!

As a woman of His Word, God is pouring His wisdom, instruction, and truth into your life. But the things He is teaching you are not just for you—they are for others, too. Your children, your co-workers, your friends and family. God is preparing you to teach others.

But there's more, because as you grow in God's grace and knowledge, He has a very specific group of people He is calling you to reach and teach…and girl, they need you bad. Let's find out who they are and the curriculum God wants you to teach.

4. Read Titus 2:3–5, and answer the following questions:

   a. Who has God called to teach and what qualities must they possess (verse 3)?

   b. What specific group does God identify to be trained and taught (verse 4)?

   c. What specific curriculum has God chosen for this teaching (verses 4–5)?

   d. How does this curriculum parallel the characteristics of the Ideal Woman?

5. Circle your answer to the following questions:

   a. Are you currently fulfilling the Titus 2:3–5 command?

      Yes   No

   b. Are you currently preparing to fulfill the Titus 2:3–5 command?

      Yes   No

c. Are you growing consistently in your knowledge of God and His Word?

Yes   No

How does an Ideal Woman become an Ideal Woman? By God's grace, of course, and by the example, influence, and teaching of godly older women. How I pray today's lesson has awakened the desire within you not only to become an Ideal Woman, but to prepare and teach the next generation to become Ideal Women, too.

6. Who has God placed in your life to receive wisdom and spiritual training? Record their names, then bow your head and ask God to give you the wisdom and specific instruction they need. Most importantly, commit to make His love your primary message and motive.

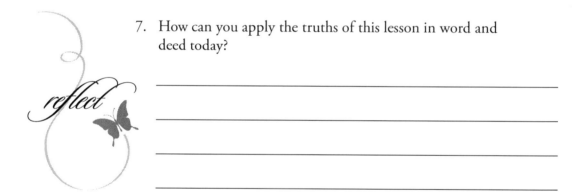

7. How can you apply the truths of this lesson in word and deed today?

_____

_____

_____

_____

DAY FIVE

1. For the past six weeks, you have been praying for wisdom using scriptures from Proverbs. But today's scripture is different. It is from the New Testament. The words were spoken by Jesus, and He is speaking about wisdom. A wise woman's life is a witness to others that God's way, the way of wisdom, is the right way. Praise and thank Him today for the wisdom He has given to you, and ask Him to use your life to point others to Him.

> *But wisdom is shown to be right by the lives of those who follow it.*
> —Luke 7:35

It is our final day of study together. We made it to the finish line, sister! I hope you have enjoyed getting to know the five females from Proverbs as much as I have. But more than that, I hope you have learned what it takes to become a true beauty, a biblical beauty.

Your study will be light today. I want to give you some extra time to reflect back over the past six weeks and praise the Father for all that He has taught you. Thank you, thank you, precious sister, for your hunger for God's Word and for your commitment to spend time studying it with me. May you enjoy and experience the pleasure of His presence as you meet with Him today.

2. Read Proverbs 31:30–31, and answer the following questions:

   a. The covers of fashion magazines, the spokespeople on infomercials, the celebrities and beauty gurus all promise the same thing: secrets to beauty. They've got potions, programs, and products galore to make you beautiful. But what is the real truth about beauty (verse 30)?

c. What is the "payoff" for biblical beauty (verses 30b–31)?

3. Does the Ideal Woman epitomize all of the best traits of biblical beauty? Find out by checking the box beside each true statement.

   ❏ She's morally pure.

   ❏ She's prudent and discreet.

   ❏ She's respectful toward her husband and speaks 3B.

   ❏ She's adored and captivated by her husband.

   ❏ She's virtuous, industrious, and she ministers to others.

4. As your final assignment in this study, take time to praise and thank God for the primary principles He has taught you over the past six weeks. Flip slowly through each lesson in this workbook and review how He spoke to you through the Immoral Woman, the Indiscreet Woman, the Irritating Woman, the Captivating Woman, and the Ideal Woman. As you review each lesson, complete the following prayer that corresponds with it. Let this be a sweet time of fellowship and overflowing praise to the Lord.

   Father, thank you for speaking to me as I studied the Immoral Woman. I praise and thank you for specifically showing me…

Father, thank you for speaking to me as I studied the Indiscreet Woman.
I praise and thank you for specifically showing me…

Father, thank you for speaking to me as I studied the Irritating Woman.
I praise and thank you for specifically showing me…

Father, thank you for speaking to me as I studied the Captivating Woman.
I praise and thank you for specifically showing me…

Father, thank you for speaking to me as I studied the Ideal Woman.
I praise and thank you for specifically showing me…

At the conclusion of each lesson, I have shared some real-life biblical beauties with you. But just like Proverbs, I have saved the best for last.

You see, I was raised by an Ideal Woman. Her name is Julia McKay. Virtuous, industrious, energetic and strong, she raised my four brothers and me mostly by herself. I am sure Mother grew weary as she shouldered the load of raising a large family while Daddy traveled as an evangelist. But she did it. Day by day, she just did it.

And while she did it, she cooked and cleaned, washed the laundry and ironed, shopped and kept the pantry filled (an almost impossible task with four boys). She oversaw our homework and read to us, got us to church almost every time the doors were open, worked in the yard and gardened, all the while chauffeuring us to piano lessons, football practice, and baseball games.

But it was not until I got older that I realized the most important thing Mother had done for us: "She (opened) her mouth in wisdom, and the teaching of kindness (was) on her tongue" (Proverbs 31:26 *NASB*). Somehow in the midst of those hectic, busy days, Mother took snatches of time to teach us eternal truths that took root and continue to bear fruit.

Mother was not and is not perfect (she would want you to know that). Yet she is the most biblically beautiful woman I know. What a privilege to have the joy of concluding this Bible study by rising up and calling her blessed…and by asking God to raise up many, many more just like her. Like *you*. My sister, take what you've learned these past six weeks, and continue becoming the biblically beautiful woman God created you to be. I am soooo proud of you!

Week Six • BECOMING AN IDEAL WOMAN

An Ideal Woman in the making is *becoming*:

1. A _____, valuable help to others. *Prov. 31:11–12*

2. A _____-_____ and a hard worker. *Prov. 31:13, 17, 19, 27*

3. A skilled _____ and servant to her family.
    Prov. 31:14–15, 21–23

4. An organized _____ and overseer. *Prov. 31:15, 21, 27*

5. A wise _____ and good steward. *Prov. 31:16, 18*

6. A gracious _____ to those in need. *Prov. 31:20*

7. An excellent _____. *Prov. 31:24,18*

8. A strong, dignified, _____ woman. *Prov. 31:21, 25*

9. A wise, kind _____, educator, and encourager.
    Prov. 31:26

10. A woman who _____ God and gives Him
    priority. *Prov. 31:30, 28*

NOTES:

Week Three
[1] Warren Baker, Eugene Carpenter, *The Complete Word Study Dictionary Old Testament* (Chattanooga, TN: AMG Publishers, 2003), 405.

[2] Ibid.

Week Four
[3] Spiros Zodhiates, *The Complete Word Study Dictionary New Testament* (Chattanooga, TN: AMG Publishers, 1993), 62.

[4] Ibid, 1031.

[5] Ibid, 1469.

[6] Ibid.

[7] Annie Chapman, *The Mother-in-Law Dance: Can Two Women Love the Same Man and Still Get Along?* (Eugene, Oregon: Harvest House Publishers, 2004), 37.

[8] James Strong, *Strong's Exhaustive Concordance* (Iowa Falls, Iowa: Riverside Book and Bible House), 113.

Week Five
[9] Warren Baker, *The Complete Word Study Old Testament* (Chattanooga, TN: AMG Publishers, 1994), 298.

[10] Warren Baker, *The Complete Word Study Dictionary Old Testament* (Chattanooga, TN: AMG Publishers, 2003), 21.

[11] Ibid, 354.

[12] Warren Baker, *The Complete Word Study Old Testament*, 2371.

[13] Linda Dillow and Lorraine Pintus, *Intimate Issues* (Colorado Springs, CO: Waterbrook Press, 2002), 18.

[14] Ibid, 203.

Week Six
[15] Warren Baker, *The Complete Word Study Dictionary Old Testament* (Chattanooga, TN: AMG Publishers, 2003), 334.

[16] Ibid.

[17] Sandra Felton, *The Messies Manual: A Complete Guide to Bringing Order and Beauty to Your Home* (Grand Rapids, MI: Fleming H. Revell, 2005), 86.

[18] Ibid, 91.

[19] Ibid.

[20] Warren Baker, *The Complete Word Study Old Testament* (Chattanooga, TN: AMG Publishers, 1994), 2315.

[21] Ibid, 2380.

[22] Ibid, 2317.

[23] Ibid.

[24] Warren Baker, *The Complete Word Study Dictionary Old Testament*, 360.

 **PRIORITY**

Visit Priority's website to learn more about Bible studies by Laurie Cole. Discover workbooks, videos, and leader guides that will encourage and equip you to give God priority!

Beauty by The Book *for Teens*
Bible Study
Learn what true beauty really looks like in this fun, friendly 7-week study from Proverbs.

Beauty by THE BOOK
Bible Study
Discover the do's and don'ts of Biblical beauty in this practical 7-week study from Proverbs.

The Temple
Bible Study
Priority's *"you glo, girl"* 11-week Bible study will help you discover how to **glo**–glorify God.

There is a Season
Bible Study
An 11-week study for women, designed to help you experience contentment in every season of life.

*P*WARRIOR *Princess*
Video only, no homework Bible study. Spiritual warfare is real, and you are on the front lines! Discover how to defeat the enemy and experience victory.

are you a DISCIPLE?
Bible Study
All disciples are Christians, but all Christians are *not* disciples. Become a disciple in this 8-week Bible study.

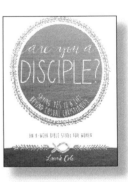

Connect with LAURIE AND PRIORITY

Encouraging Women to Give God Glory & Priority

The Priority blog is dedicated to busy women everywhere who may have a million things going on, but still want to make God the #1 thing. It can be done, and Laurie's guilt-free teaching and resources will help you do it. You really *can* give Him priority—even in your busy life!

priorityministries.com/christian-womens-blog

Support PRIORITY

Supporting Priority Ministries

Priority Partners believe in the mission of Priority Ministries and support it with their generous financial gifts. Would you prayerfully consider becoming a Partner and helping us reach and teach women to love God most and seek Him first?

Become a monthly or one-time donor. Either way, your financial gifts provide vital support for this ministry! For more information about becoming a Priority Partner, visit our website: **priorityministries.com/donations**

Priority Ministries is a non-profit 501(c)3 organization.
Your gift is tax deductible.

Made in the USA
Columbia, SC
13 March 2023

13723891R00080